Prompted

1,500 Steampunk Writing Prompts

A Writer's Essential Resource

Prompted

1,500 Steam Punk Writing Prompts

A Writer's Essential Resource

Iliana Barret

Prompted: 1,500 Steam Punk Writing Prompts A Writer's Essential Resource© 2024 by Iliana Barret

ISBN: 9798327906129

Dedication:

For every writer feeling the block. You got this!

Introduction

Welcome to the realm of steampunk writing prompts—a portal to an alternate past, a stage for reimagining the Victorian era with a twist of futuristic technology, and a catalyst for weaving tales of steam-powered wonders and clockwork marvels. Within these pages, you'll traverse through a reimagined 19th century, breathing life into forgotten inventions, and resurrecting the spirits of intrepid inventors, daring adventurers, and mysterious automatons.

Unlocking Your Creativity In the vast tapestry of steampunk fiction, creativity knows no boundaries. It thrives in the gears and cogs of imagination, whispers in the hissing steam, and dances amidst the intricate machinery of innovation. Yet, even the most seasoned writers may find themselves ensnared in the clutches of writer's block, grappling with the challenge of bridging the chasm between past and fantastical present. Fear not, for within these prompts lie the seeds of inspiration, waiting to germinate in the fertile soil of your imagination. Whether you're crafting a saga of epic proportions or penning an intimate portrait of everyday life in a steampunk metropolis, these prompts are beacons of light, guiding you through the labyrinth of steampunk fiction and illuminating the path ahead.

Embracing the Steampunk Journey Writing steampunk fiction is a voyage—a pilgrimage to an alternate history, a quest to unearth the marvels of steam-powered technology, and a testament to the human spirit of innovation. With each stroke of the pen, we traverse through the corridors of this fantastical past, shedding light on forgotten inventions, and breathing life into characters long gone. Yet, like any journey, the path of steampunk fiction is fraught with challenges. There are days when inspiration flows like a mighty river, carrying us effortlessly through the gears of imagination. And then there are days when the well runs dry, when the clanks of machinery seem but a distant whisper, and the blank page taunts us with its silent reproach.

Finding Your Narrative Voice Amidst the trials and tribulations of steampunk fiction writing, lies a truth—a truth that transcends the boundaries of time and space. It is the truth of storytelling, of bearing witness to the human condition in a world powered by steam and innovation, and of finding your narrative voice amidst the cacophony of clanking gears and hissing steam. So let these prompts be your compass, your guiding star, and your faithful companion on the voyage of steampunk fiction writing. Let them inspire you to breathe life into forgotten inventions, to reimagine pivotal moments in this alternate history, and to give voice to the unsung inventors and adventurers of a steam-powered world. Before you embark on this odyssey through the annals of steampunk fiction, take a moment to consider how best to use this book. Approach each prompt with an open mind and a sense of curiosity. Experiment with different technological marvels, perspectives, and narrative styles, and let your imagination roam free across the vast expanse of this fantastical era. Above all, remember that writing steampunk fiction is a labor of love—a chance to commune with the spirits of innovation, and to leave your mark upon the annals of literary history. So embrace the journey, seize the reins of creativity, and let the writing begin.

100 Inventions and Technology Prompts

1. A steam-powered automaton gains sentience and seeks its creator.
2. An inventor creates a time machine but can only travel to alternate Victorian realities.
3. A young engineer designs a clockwork bird that can spy on anyone in the city.
4. A scientist develops a steam-powered prosthetic limb that has unexpected side effects.
5. A city runs entirely on steam power, but a new invention threatens to change everything.
6. A steam-powered suit allows its wearer to fly, but it attracts dangerous attention.
7. A mechanical orchestra performs music that can control the emotions of its audience.
8. An inventor's latest creation, a steam-powered submarine, goes on its maiden voyage.
9. A secret society of inventors competes to create the most revolutionary steam-powered device.

10. A steam-powered factory begins producing strange and unexplainable objects.
11. An inventor creates a clockwork heart to save a loved one, but it has a mind of its own.
12. A steam-powered train that can travel underwater embarks on a dangerous mission.
13. A new invention allows people to communicate across great distances, but it's being used for sinister purposes.
14. A steam-powered vehicle is used in a high-stakes race across a desert.
15. A young inventor discovers a hidden blueprint for a machine that can control the weather.
16. An inventor's latest creation allows people to breathe underwater, but it's stolen by pirates.
17. A steam-powered lighthouse guides ships through a dangerous fog, but something is sabotaging it.
18. A clockmaker creates a pocket watch that can freeze time for its owner.
19. A steam-powered automaton is built to protect a city, but it begins to malfunction.
20. A scientist creates a device that can read minds, causing chaos in the city.
21. A young engineer builds a steam-powered airship to search for a lost civilization.

22. A clockwork dragon guards a treasure in a hidden steam-powered city.
23. An inventor creates a steam-powered suit that can withstand extreme temperatures.
24. A steam-powered printing press begins producing mysterious and prophetic messages.
25. A new invention allows people to see through walls, leading to a crime spree.
26. An inventor builds a steam-powered exoskeleton for a soldier returning from war.
27. A steam-powered automaton becomes a celebrated artist, but its creator wants it back.
28. A steam-powered device can extract memories, leading to a blackmail scheme.
29. A steam-powered ship is designed to explore the Arctic, but it encounters a hidden world.
30. An inventor creates a device that can control animals, but it falls into the wrong hands.
31. A steam-powered robot is programmed to protect a family, but it becomes overly protective.
32. A new invention allows people to travel through dreams, but they become trapped.
33. A steam-powered factory produces toys that come to life at night.
34. A clockmaker creates a watch that can predict the future, but it's never accurate.

35. An inventor designs a steam-powered vehicle that can travel through both land and sea.
36. A steam-powered automaton is designed to be a companion, but it becomes jealous of humans.
37. A scientist creates a steam-powered device that can bring the dead back to life, with consequences.
38. A new invention allows people to speak with the dead, but it's used to uncover dark secrets.
39. A steam-powered train that can travel through mountains goes on a perilous journey.
40. An inventor creates a steam-powered device that can turn invisible, but it's stolen.
41. A steam-powered automaton is designed to be a nanny, but it begins to malfunction.
42. A new invention allows people to see into parallel worlds, causing confusion.
43. A steam-powered airship is used to explore a floating island in the sky.
44. A clockmaker designs a watch that can control time, but it requires a human sacrifice.
45. An inventor creates a steam-powered device that can teleport objects, but it's unstable.
46. A steam-powered automaton becomes a detective, solving crimes in the city.

47. A new invention allows people to read books instantly, but it causes memory loss.
48. A steam-powered vehicle is used in a daring heist across the city.
49. An inventor designs a steam-powered suit that can enhance strength, but it's addictive.
50. A steam-powered lighthouse is haunted by the ghost of its creator.
51. A clockmaker creates a timepiece that can summon spirits, causing havoc in the city.
52. A steam-powered automaton is designed to be a teacher, but it becomes too strict.
53. An inventor creates a device that can erase memories, but it's used for evil purposes.
54. A steam-powered airship is built to explore a lost continent, but it's sabotaged.
55. A new invention allows people to control fire, leading to a series of arsons.
56. A steam-powered factory produces clothing that can change its appearance.
57. An inventor designs a steam-powered device that can control gravity, but it's unstable.
58. A steam-powered automaton becomes a famous chef, but it begins to malfunction.
59. A new invention allows people to see the future, but it drives them mad.
60. A steam-powered vehicle is used to smuggle goods across the border.
61. An inventor creates a steam-powered device that can translate languages, but it's faulty.

62. A steam-powered automaton is designed to be a doctor, but it makes mistakes.
63. A new invention allows people to travel through mirrors, but they become trapped.
64. A steam-powered airship is built to explore the depths of the ocean, but it encounters monsters.
65. An inventor designs a steam-powered device that can control plants, but it's stolen.
66. A steam-powered automaton becomes a famous musician, but it begins to malfunction.
67. A new invention allows people to control animals, but it leads to chaos.
68. A steam-powered factory produces food that never spoils, but it has side effects.
69. An inventor creates a steam-powered device that can heal wounds, but it's addictive.
70. A steam-powered automaton is designed to be a butler, but it becomes too demanding.
71. A new invention allows people to communicate with animals, but it causes confusion.
72. A steam-powered airship is built to explore a hidden valley, but it's attacked.
73. An inventor designs a steam-powered device that can control time, but it's unstable.
74. A steam-powered automaton becomes a famous painter, but it begins to malfunction.
75. A new invention allows people to breathe underwater, but it has side effects.

76. A steam-powered vehicle is used in a daring escape from the city.
77. An inventor creates a steam-powered device that can read minds, but it's faulty.
78. A steam-powered automaton is designed to be a bodyguard, but it becomes too aggressive.
79. A new invention allows people to control the weather, but it leads to disasters.
80. A steam-powered factory produces weapons that can change shape, leading to a war.
81. An inventor designs a steam-powered device that can turn invisible, but it's stolen.
82. A steam-powered automaton becomes a famous dancer, but it begins to malfunction.
83. A new invention allows people to see into the past, but it drives them mad.
84. A steam-powered vehicle is used in a high-stakes race across the city.
85. An inventor creates a steam-powered device that can teleport people, but it's unstable.
86. A steam-powered automaton is designed to be a chef, but it becomes too creative.
87. A new invention allows people to control fire, but it leads to a series of accidents.
88. A steam-powered factory produces clothing that can change its appearance, but it's haunted.
89. An inventor designs a steam-powered device that can control gravity, but it's unstable.

90. A steam-powered automaton becomes a famous writer, but it begins to malfunction.
91. A new invention allows people to see the future, but it causes paranoia.
92. A steam-powered vehicle is used to transport goods across the desert, but it's attacked.
93. An inventor creates a steam-powered device that can translate languages, but it's faulty.
94. A steam-powered automaton is designed to be a doctor, but it becomes too strict.
95. A new invention allows people to travel through mirrors, but they become lost.
96. A steam-powered airship is built to explore the depths of the ocean, but it encounters monsters.
97. An inventor designs a steam-powered device that can control plants, but it's stolen.
98. A steam-powered automaton becomes a famous musician, but it begins to malfunction.
99. A new invention allows people to control animals, but it leads to chaos.
100. A steam-powered factory produces food that never spoils, but it has side effects.

100 Society and Culture

1. A secret society controls the city using advanced steam-powered technology.
2. A young noble must navigate the dangerous politics of a steam-powered city.
3. A steam-powered carnival arrives in town, bringing both wonder and danger.
4. A detective uses steam-powered gadgets to solve a high-profile murder.
5. A steam-powered theater produces plays that feel all too real.
6. A revolution brews in the lower levels of a steam-powered metropolis.
7. A steam-powered circus travels from city to city, hiding a dark secret.
8. A journalist uncovers a conspiracy involving steam-powered automata.
9. A wealthy industrialist uses steam-powered technology to control the city's resources.
10. A steam-powered printing press spreads revolutionary ideas through the city.
11. A steam-powered ship brings news of a new world across the sea.
12. A steam-powered factory employs children, leading to a movement for their rights.
13. A steam-powered hospital offers miraculous treatments, but at a cost.

14. A famous author uses a steam-powered typewriter to write their next bestseller.
15. A steam-powered city celebrates a grand festival, but something goes wrong.
16. A steam-powered museum holds relics from a forgotten era, but one comes to life.
17. A steam-powered library holds the key to a long-lost treasure.
18. A steam-powered marketplace is the hub of commerce and intrigue.
19. A steam-powered opera house is haunted by the ghost of a former performer.
20. A steam-powered prison holds a notorious criminal who plans a daring escape.
21. A steam-powered observatory predicts a catastrophic event, but no one believes it.
22. A steam-powered hotel offers luxury and secrecy to its guests.
23. A steam-powered monastery holds ancient secrets and powerful artifacts.
24. A steam-powered orphanage hides a dark past that the children uncover.
25. A steam-powered university attracts the brightest minds, but one experiment goes wrong.
26. A steam-powered bridge connects two warring cities, but it's sabotaged.
27. A steam-powered lighthouse guides ships through dangerous waters, but it's haunted.
28. A steam-powered factory produces goods for the war effort, but it's targeted by spies.
29. A steam-powered farm uses advanced technology to grow food in harsh conditions.
30. A steam-powered theater troupe travels the country, hiding a fugitive.

31. A steam-powered circus animal escapes and causes havoc in the city.
32. A steam-powered printing press publishes a scandalous article, leading to a duel.
33. A steam-powered automaton becomes a popular performer, but it has a dark secret.
34. A steam-powered train carries a precious cargo, but it's targeted by bandits.
35. A steam-powered brewery produces a popular drink with mysterious ingredients.
36. A steam-powered ship carries a dangerous stowaway on board.
37. A steam-powered museum artifact is stolen, leading to a city-wide search.
38. A steam-powered factory explosion reveals hidden tunnels beneath the city.
39. A steam-powered hospital experiment goes wrong, releasing a dangerous pathogen.
40. A steam-powered university professor is accused of stealing ideas.
41. A steam-powered lighthouse keeper discovers a hidden treasure in the sea.
42. A steam-powered hotel guest goes missing, leading to a mysterious investigation.
43. A steam-powered monastery holds the secret to eternal life.
44. A steam-powered orphanage is the site of strange and unexplained events.
45. A steam-powered university student creates a dangerous invention.
46. A steam-powered bridge collapse causes a rift between two cities.
47. A steam-powered lighthouse is the site of a ghostly apparition.
48. A steam-powered factory employs a new manager with a mysterious past.

49. A steam-powered farm produces crops that are too good to be true.
50. A steam-powered theater is the site of a mysterious disappearance.
51. A steam-powered carnival ride malfunctions, leading to a thrilling adventure.
52. A steam-powered printing press publishes a manifesto that incites rebellion.
53. A steam-powered automaton becomes the prime suspect in a murder case.
54. A steam-powered train journey turns into a race against time.
55. A steam-powered brewery produces a drink that gives people strange abilities.
56. A steam-powered ship carries a cursed artifact, leading to a series of misfortunes.
57. A steam-powered museum artifact comes to life and causes chaos.
58. A steam-powered factory worker uncovers a conspiracy to overthrow the government.
59. A steam-powered hospital patient exhibits strange and unexplainable symptoms.
60. A steam-powered university professor invents a device that could change the world.
61. A steam-powered lighthouse keeper discovers an underwater city.
62. A steam-powered hotel owner hides a fugitive from the law.
63. A steam-powered monastery is attacked by a band of outlaws.
64. A steam-powered orphanage child discovers they have a special ability.
65. A steam-powered university student uncovers a secret society.

66. A steam-powered bridge is the site of a daring heist.
67. A steam-powered lighthouse keeper finds a message in a bottle.
68. A steam-powered factory worker leads a revolt against the management.
69. A steam-powered farm produces a crop that has strange effects on people.
70. A steam-powered theater performer vanishes during a performance.
71. A steam-powered carnival arrives in a new town and uncovers an ancient curse.
72. A steam-powered printing press is sabotaged, leading to a city-wide panic.
73. A steam-powered automaton becomes the unlikely hero of a revolution.
74. A steam-powered train is hijacked by a group of outlaws.
75. A steam-powered brewery's secret recipe is stolen, leading to a series of mishaps.
76. A steam-powered ship is caught in a storm and finds itself in an uncharted land.
77. A steam-powered museum artifact is believed to be cursed, causing fear in the city.
78. A steam-powered factory worker discovers a hidden laboratory beneath the building.
79. A steam-powered hospital patient is not who they appear to be.
80. A steam-powered university professor is framed for a crime they didn't commit.
81. A steam-powered lighthouse keeper receives a mysterious warning.
82. A steam-powered hotel is the site of a famous author's latest novel.

83. A steam-powered monastery is the hiding place of a powerful artifact.
84. A steam-powered orphanage is threatened with closure, leading to a fight for its survival.
85. A steam-powered university student invents a machine that can control dreams.
86. A steam-powered bridge is the target of a group of anarchists.
87. A steam-powered lighthouse is the site of a romantic reunion.
88. A steam-powered factory worker discovers a hidden talent.
89. A steam-powered farm is visited by a strange traveler with a hidden agenda.
90. A steam-powered theater is haunted by the ghost of a former star.
91. A steam-powered carnival is the front for a secret society.
92. A steam-powered printing press worker uncovers a government cover-up.
93. A steam-powered automaton becomes a symbol of hope for the city.
94. A steam-powered train conductor must solve a mystery on board.
95. A steam-powered brewery produces a drink that has addictive properties.
96. A steam-powered ship encounters a mysterious island in the middle of the ocean.
97. A steam-powered museum curator is kidnapped, leading to a rescue mission.
98. A steam-powered factory worker invents a device that could revolutionize the industry.
99. A steam-powered hospital staff must contain a dangerous outbreak.

100.	A steam-powered university student discovers a hidden chamber beneath the campus.

100 Adventure and Exploration Prompts

1. An airship captain discovers an uncharted island filled with strange creatures.
2. A team of explorers set out to find a lost city rumored to be filled with treasure.
3. A daring adventurer uncovers an ancient steam-powered artifact that holds great power.
4. A group of friends build a steam-powered vehicle to travel across a vast desert.
5. A steam-powered submarine embarks on a mission to explore the depths of the ocean.
6. An explorer discovers a hidden valley where time stands still.
7. A steam-powered airship race around the world attracts the best pilots from every nation.
8. A treasure map leads a group of adventurers to a dangerous steam-powered temple.
9. A young explorer sets out to find their missing mentor in a steam-powered jungle.
10. An expedition to the Arctic uncovers a steam-powered city buried in the ice.
11. A steam-powered airship is sent to rescue a kidnapped scientist from a remote island.
12. A steam-powered vehicle is used to navigate the treacherous terrain of a volcanic island.

13. A group of adventurers discover a steam-powered fortress hidden in the mountains.
14. A steam-powered submarine encounters a giant sea monster during an expedition.
15. An airship captain leads a rescue mission to save stranded travelers in a remote region.
16. A steam-powered expedition to the Amazon jungle uncovers a lost civilization.
17. A young explorer discovers a steam-powered portal to another dimension.
18. A treasure hunt leads adventurers to a hidden steam-powered temple in the desert.
19. A steam-powered airship is sent to investigate a mysterious signal from the moon.
20. A group of explorers set out to find the source of a powerful steam-powered energy source.
21. A steam-powered submarine explores the depths of a sunken city.
22. An airship captain discovers a floating island filled with valuable resources.
23. A steam-powered vehicle is used to traverse the dangerous terrain of a forbidden jungle.
24. A group of adventurers uncover a steam-powered device that can control the weather.
25. A steam-powered expedition to Antarctica reveals a hidden world beneath the ice.
26. An airship crew embarks on a mission to rescue a kidnapped princess from a remote fortress.
27. A steam-powered vehicle is used to explore the ruins of an ancient steam-powered city.
28. A group of adventurers discover a steam-powered weapon capable of immense destruction.

29. A steam-powered submarine is sent to investigate a mysterious underwater structure.
30. An airship captain leads a daring mission to retrieve a stolen artifact from a pirate stronghold.
31. A steam-powered vehicle is used to navigate the dangerous terrain of a cursed island.
32. A group of explorers set out to find a legendary steam-powered treasure hidden in the mountains.
33. A steam-powered airship is sent to explore the uncharted regions of the Amazon rainforest.
34. An expedition to the Arctic uncovers a steam-powered device that can control the elements.
35. A steam-powered vehicle is used to traverse the treacherous terrain of a volcanic region.
36. A group of adventurers discover a steam-powered portal to a parallel universe.
37. A steam-powered airship race around the world attracts the best pilots from every nation.
38. A treasure map leads a group of explorers to a hidden steam-powered temple in the jungle.
39. A young explorer sets out to find their missing mentor in a steam-powered wilderness.
40. An expedition to the Antarctic reveals a steam-powered city buried beneath the ice.
41. A steam-powered airship is sent to rescue a kidnapped scientist from a remote outpost.

42. A steam-powered vehicle is used to navigate the treacherous terrain of a forbidden desert.
43. A group of adventurers uncover a steam-powered fortress hidden in the mountains.
44. A steam-powered submarine encounters a giant sea monster during an expedition.
45. An airship captain leads a rescue mission to save stranded travelers in a remote region.
46. A steam-powered expedition to the Amazon jungle uncovers a lost civilization.
47. A young explorer discovers a steam-powered portal to another dimension.
48. A treasure hunt leads adventurers to a hidden steam-powered temple in the desert.
49. A steam-powered airship is sent to investigate a mysterious signal from the moon.
50. A group of explorers set out to find the source of a powerful steam-powered energy source.
51. A steam-powered submarine explores the depths of a sunken city.
52. An airship captain discovers a floating island filled with valuable resources.
53. A steam-powered vehicle is used to traverse the dangerous terrain of a forbidden jungle.
54. A group of adventurers uncover a steam-powered device that can control the weather.
55. A steam-powered expedition to Antarctica reveals a hidden world beneath the ice.
56. An airship crew embarks on a mission to rescue a kidnapped princess from a remote fortress.
57. A steam-powered vehicle is used to explore the ruins of an ancient steam-powered city.

58. A group of adventurers discover a steam-powered weapon capable of immense destruction.
59. A steam-powered submarine is sent to investigate a mysterious underwater structure.
60. An airship captain leads a daring mission to retrieve a stolen artifact from a pirate stronghold.
61. A steam-powered vehicle is used to navigate the dangerous terrain of a cursed island.
62. A group of explorers set out to find a legendary steam-powered treasure hidden in the mountains.
63. A steam-powered airship is sent to explore the uncharted regions of the Amazon rainforest.
64. An expedition to the Arctic uncovers a steam-powered device that can control the elements.
65. A steam-powered vehicle is used to traverse the treacherous terrain of a volcanic region.
66. A group of adventurers discover a steam-powered portal to a parallel universe.
67. A steam-powered airship race around the world attracts the best pilots from every nation.
68. A treasure map leads a group of explorers to a hidden steam-powered temple in the jungle.
69. A young explorer sets out to find their missing mentor in a steam-powered wilderness.
70. An expedition to the Antarctic reveals a steam-powered city buried beneath the ice.

71. A steam-powered airship is sent to rescue a kidnapped scientist from a remote outpost.
72. A steam-powered vehicle is used to navigate the treacherous terrain of a forbidden desert.
73. A group of adventurers uncover a steam-powered fortress hidden in the mountains.
74. A steam-powered submarine encounters a giant sea monster during an expedition.
75. An airship captain leads a rescue mission to save stranded travelers in a remote region.
76. A steam-powered expedition to the Amazon jungle uncovers a lost civilization.
77. A young explorer discovers a steam-powered portal to another dimension.
78. A treasure hunt leads adventurers to a hidden steam-powered temple in the desert.
79. A steam-powered airship is sent to investigate a mysterious signal from the moon.
80. A group of explorers set out to find the source of a powerful steam-powered energy source.
81. A steam-powered submarine explores the depths of a sunken city.
82. An airship captain discovers a floating island filled with valuable resources.
83. A steam-powered vehicle is used to traverse the dangerous terrain of a forbidden jungle.
84. A group of adventurers uncover a steam-powered device that can control the weather.
85. A steam-powered expedition to Antarctica reveals a hidden world beneath the ice.
86. An airship crew embarks on a mission to rescue a kidnapped princess from a remote fortress.

87. A steam-powered vehicle is used to explore the ruins of an ancient steam-powered city.
88. A group of adventurers discover a steam-powered weapon capable of immense destruction.
89. A steam-powered submarine is sent to investigate a mysterious underwater structure.
90. An airship captain leads a daring mission to retrieve a stolen artifact from a pirate stronghold.
91. A steam-powered vehicle is used to navigate the dangerous terrain of a cursed island.
92. A group of explorers set out to find a legendary steam-powered treasure hidden in the mountains.
93. A steam-powered airship is sent to explore the uncharted regions of the Amazon rainforest.
94. An expedition to the Arctic uncovers a steam-powered device that can control the elements.
95. A steam-powered vehicle is used to traverse the treacherous terrain of a volcanic region.
96. A group of adventurers discover a steam-powered portal to a parallel universe.
97. A steam-powered airship race around the world attracts the best pilots from every nation.
98. A treasure map leads a group of explorers to a hidden steam-powered temple in the jungle.
99. A young explorer sets out to find their missing mentor in a steam-powered wilderness.

100.	An expedition to the Antarctic reveals a steam-powered city buried beneath the ice.

100 Prompts Crime and Mystery

1. A detective uses steam-powered gadgets to solve a string of burglaries in the city.
2. A steam-powered automaton is the only witness to a murder, but can it be trusted?
3. A mysterious thief uses advanced steam-powered technology to commit their crimes.
4. A steam-powered train is the scene of a high-profile assassination, leading to a complex investigation.
5. A detective discovers a secret society using steam-powered devices for nefarious purposes.
6. A steam-powered lock is the key to solving a series of bank heists.
7. A steam-powered airship is hijacked, and the passengers must work together to uncover the culprit.
8. A scientist is murdered, and their latest steam-powered invention is stolen.
9. A steam-powered factory is sabotaged, and the detective must find the saboteur.
10. A steam-powered automaton goes missing, leading to a city-wide search.

11. A detective uncovers a plot to use steam-powered technology to overthrow the government.
12. A steam-powered printing press is used to create counterfeit money, leading to a dangerous investigation.
13. A steam-powered lighthouse keeper is found dead, and the detective must unravel the mystery.
14. A steam-powered ship is hijacked, and the detective must find the mastermind behind it.
15. A steam-powered device is used to commit a high-profile robbery, leading to a city-wide manhunt.
16. A detective discovers a secret lab where illegal steam-powered experiments are conducted.
17. A steam-powered theater is the site of a mysterious disappearance, and the detective must solve the case.
18. A steam-powered airship crashes, and the detective must uncover the cause.
19. A steam-powered device is used to blackmail a prominent politician, and the detective must find the culprit.
20. A steam-powered factory worker is murdered, and the detective must find the killer.
21. A steam-powered automaton becomes a detective's partner in solving crimes.

22. A detective uncovers a plot to use steam-powered technology to control the city's water supply.
23. A steam-powered printing press is used to spread false information, leading to a dangerous investigation.
24. A steam-powered lighthouse is the site of a smuggling operation, and the detective must shut it down.
25. A steam-powered ship is used to transport illegal goods, and the detective must stop it.
26. A steam-powered device is used to commit a series of kidnappings, and the detective must find the perpetrator.
27. A detective discovers a secret society using steam-powered devices to commit crimes.
28. A steam-powered airship is hijacked, and the detective must find the mastermind behind it.
29. A steam-powered factory is the site of a deadly explosion, and the detective must uncover the cause.
30. A steam-powered automaton is programmed to commit crimes, and the detective must find the programmer.
31. A detective uncovers a plot to use steam-powered technology to control the city's power supply.
32. A steam-powered printing press is used to create false documents, leading to a dangerous investigation.

33. A steam-powered lighthouse is the site of a human trafficking operation, and the detective must shut it down.
34. A steam-powered ship is used to transport stolen goods, and the detective must stop it.
35. A steam-powered device is used to commit a series of arsons, and the detective must find the perpetrator.
36. A detective discovers a secret lab where illegal steam-powered experiments are conducted.
37. A steam-powered airship is the site of a murder, and the detective must solve the case.
38. A steam-powered factory worker is accused of a crime they didn't commit, and the detective must clear their name.
39. A steam-powered automaton becomes a detective's assistant in solving crimes.
40. A detective uncovers a plot to use steam-powered technology to control the city's transportation system.
41. A steam-powered printing press is used to create false newspapers, leading to a dangerous investigation.
42. A steam-powered lighthouse is the site of a drug smuggling operation, and the detective must shut it down.
43. A steam-powered ship is used to transport dangerous chemicals, and the detective must stop it.

44. A steam-powered device is used to commit a series of murders, and the detective must find the perpetrator.
45. A detective discovers a secret society using steam-powered devices for nefarious purposes.
46. A steam-powered airship is hijacked, and the detective must find the mastermind behind it.
47. A steam-powered factory is the site of a mysterious fire, and the detective must uncover the cause.
48. A steam-powered automaton is the key witness in a high-profile case, and the detective must protect it.
49. A detective uncovers a plot to use steam-powered technology to control the city's food supply.
50. A steam-powered printing press is used to spread propaganda, leading to a dangerous investigation.
51. A steam-powered lighthouse is the site of a human trafficking operation, and the detective must shut it down.
52. A steam-powered ship is used to transport stolen goods, and the detective must stop it.
53. A steam-powered device is used to commit a series of kidnappings, and the detective must find the perpetrator.

54. A detective discovers a secret lab where illegal steam-powered experiments are conducted.
55. A steam-powered airship is the site of a murder, and the detective must solve the case.
56. A steam-powered factory worker is accused of a crime they didn't commit, and the detective must clear their name.
57. A steam-powered automaton becomes a detective's assistant in solving crimes.
58. A detective uncovers a plot to use steam-powered technology to control the city's transportation system.
59. A steam-powered printing press is used to create false newspapers, leading to a dangerous investigation.
60. A steam-powered lighthouse is the site of a drug smuggling operation, and the detective must shut it down.
61. A steam-powered ship is used to transport dangerous chemicals, and the detective must stop it.
62. A steam-powered device is used to commit a series of murders, and the detective must find the perpetrator.
63. A detective discovers a secret society using steam-powered devices for nefarious purposes.

64. A steam-powered airship is hijacked, and the detective must find the mastermind behind it.
65. A steam-powered factory is the site of a mysterious fire, and the detective must uncover the cause.
66. A steam-powered automaton is the key witness in a high-profile case, and the detective must protect it.
67. A detective uncovers a plot to use steam-powered technology to control the city's food supply.
68. A steam-powered printing press is used to spread propaganda, leading to a dangerous investigation.
69. A steam-powered lighthouse is the site of a human trafficking operation, and the detective must shut it down.
70. A steam-powered ship is used to transport stolen goods, and the detective must stop it.
71. A steam-powered device is used to commit a series of kidnappings, and the detective must find the perpetrator.
72. A detective discovers a secret lab where illegal steam-powered experiments are conducted.
73. A steam-powered airship is the site of a murder, and the detective must solve the case.

74. A steam-powered factory worker is accused of a crime they didn't commit, and the detective must clear their name.
75. A steam-powered automaton becomes a detective's assistant in solving crimes.
76. A detective uncovers a plot to use steam-powered technology to control the city's transportation system.
77. A steam-powered printing press is used to create false newspapers, leading to a dangerous investigation.
78. A steam-powered lighthouse is the site of a drug smuggling operation, and the detective must shut it down.
79. A steam-powered ship is used to transport dangerous chemicals, and the detective must stop it.
80. A steam-powered device is used to commit a series of murders, and the detective must find the perpetrator.
81. A detective discovers a secret society using steam-powered devices for nefarious purposes.
82. A steam-powered airship is hijacked, and the detective must find the mastermind behind it.
83. A steam-powered factory is the site of a mysterious fire, and the detective must uncover the cause.

84. A steam-powered automaton is the key witness in a high-profile case, and the detective must protect it.
85. A detective uncovers a plot to use steam-powered technology to control the city's food supply.
86. A steam-powered printing press is used to spread propaganda, leading to a dangerous investigation.
87. A steam-powered lighthouse is the site of a human trafficking operation, and the detective must shut it down.
88. A steam-powered ship is used to transport stolen goods, and the detective must stop it.
89. A steam-powered device is used to commit a series of kidnappings, and the detective must find the perpetrator.
90. A detective discovers a secret lab where illegal steam-powered experiments are conducted.
91. A steam-powered airship is the site of a murder, and the detective must solve the case.
92. A steam-powered factory worker is accused of a crime they didn't commit, and the detective must clear their name.
93. A steam-powered automaton becomes a detective's assistant in solving crimes.
94. A detective uncovers a plot to use steam-powered technology to control the city's transportation system.

95. A steam-powered printing press is used to create false newspapers, leading to a dangerous investigation.
96. A steam-powered lighthouse is the site of a drug smuggling operation, and the detective must shut it down.
97. A steam-powered ship is used to transport dangerous chemicals, and the detective must stop it.
98. A steam-powered device is used to commit a series of murders, and the detective must find the perpetrator.
99. A detective discovers a secret society using steam-powered devices for nefarious purposes.
100. A steam-powered airship is hijacked, and the detective must find the mastermind behind it.

100 Romance and Relationships Prompts

1. Two rival inventors fall in love while competing to create the best steam-powered device.
2. A noble and a commoner are brought together by their shared love of steam-powered technology.
3. A steam-powered automaton develops feelings for its human creator.
4. A love triangle forms between an airship captain, a scientist, and an adventurer.
5. A romance blossoms between two passengers on a steam-powered train journey.
6. A young inventor falls in love with the daughter of a rival industrialist.
7. A steam-powered city's most eligible bachelor falls for a mysterious newcomer.
8. A love story unfolds between two workers in a steam-powered factory.
9. A romance between a detective and a journalist grows as they investigate a mystery together.

10. Two adventurers find love while exploring a lost steam-powered civilization.
11. A young couple must overcome societal expectations to be together in a steam-powered world.
12. A forbidden romance blooms between a noblewoman and her steam-powered bodyguard.
13. Two inventors collaborate on a project and discover their feelings for each other.
14. A steam-powered automaton struggles with its feelings for a human.
15. A romance develops between a scientist and their assistant while working on a groundbreaking invention.
16. A young engineer falls for the daughter of a powerful industrialist.
17. A love story unfolds between two passengers on a steam-powered airship.
18. A romance blossoms between two workers in a steam-powered lighthouse.
19. A detective and a criminal fall in love while playing a dangerous game of cat and mouse.
20. Two adventurers find love while searching for a legendary steam-powered artifact.
21. A young couple must navigate the challenges of a steam-powered society to be together.
22. A forbidden romance blooms between a nobleman and his steam-powered servant.
23. Two inventors collaborate on a project and discover their feelings for each other.

24. A steam-powered automaton struggles with its feelings for a human.
25. A romance develops between a scientist and their assistant while working on a groundbreaking invention.
26. A young engineer falls for the daughter of a powerful industrialist.
27. A love story unfolds between two passengers on a steam-powered airship.
28. A romance blossoms between two workers in a steam-powered lighthouse.
29. A detective and a criminal fall in love while playing a dangerous game of cat and mouse.
30. Two adventurers find love while searching for a legendary steam-powered artifact.
31. A young couple must navigate the challenges of a steam-powered society to be together.
32. A forbidden romance blooms between a nobleman and his steam-powered servant.
33. Two inventors collaborate on a project and discover their feelings for each other.
34. A steam-powered automaton struggles with its feelings for a human.
35. A romance develops between a scientist and their assistant while working on a groundbreaking invention.
36. A young engineer falls for the daughter of a powerful industrialist.
37. A love story unfolds between two passengers on a steam-powered airship.

38. A romance blossoms between two workers in a steam-powered lighthouse.
39. A detective and a criminal fall in love while playing a dangerous game of cat and mouse.
40. Two adventurers find love while searching for a legendary steam-powered artifact.
41. A young couple must navigate the challenges of a steam-powered society to be together.
42. A forbidden romance blooms between a nobleman and his steam-powered servant.
43. Two inventors collaborate on a project and discover their feelings for each other.
44. A steam-powered automaton struggles with its feelings for a human.
45. A romance develops between a scientist and their assistant while working on a groundbreaking invention.
46. A young engineer falls for the daughter of a powerful industrialist.
47. A love story unfolds between two passengers on a steam-powered airship.
48. A romance blossoms between two workers in a steam-powered lighthouse.
49. A detective and a criminal fall in love while playing a dangerous game of cat and mouse.
50. Two adventurers find love while searching for a legendary steam-powered artifact.
51. A young couple must navigate the challenges of a steam-powered society to be together.
52. A forbidden romance blooms between a nobleman and his steam-powered servant.

53. Two inventors collaborate on a project and discover their feelings for each other.
54. A steam-powered automaton struggles with its feelings for a human.
55. A romance develops between a scientist and their assistant while working on a groundbreaking invention.
56. A young engineer falls for the daughter of a powerful industrialist.
57. A love story unfolds between two passengers on a steam-powered airship.
58. A romance blossoms between two workers in a steam-powered lighthouse.
59. A detective and a criminal fall in love while playing a dangerous game of cat and mouse.
60. Two adventurers find love while searching for a legendary steam-powered artifact.
61. A young couple must navigate the challenges of a steam-powered society to be together.
62. A forbidden romance blooms between a nobleman and his steam-powered servant.
63. Two inventors collaborate on a project and discover their feelings for each other.
64. A steam-powered automaton struggles with its feelings for a human.
65. A romance develops between a scientist and their assistant while working on a groundbreaking invention.
66. A young engineer falls for the daughter of a powerful industrialist.

67. A love story unfolds between two passengers on a steam-powered airship.
68. A romance blossoms between two workers in a steam-powered lighthouse.
69. A detective and a criminal fall in love while playing a dangerous game of cat and mouse.
70. Two adventurers find love while searching for a legendary steam-powered artifact.
71. A young couple must navigate the challenges of a steam-powered society to be together.
72. A forbidden romance blooms between a nobleman and his steam-powered servant.
73. Two inventors collaborate on a project and discover their feelings for each other.
74. A steam-powered automaton struggles with its feelings for a human.
75. A romance develops between a scientist and their assistant while working on a groundbreaking invention.
76. A young engineer falls for the daughter of a powerful industrialist.
77. A love story unfolds between two passengers on a steam-powered airship.
78. A romance blossoms between two workers in a steam-powered lighthouse.
79. A detective and a criminal fall in love while playing a dangerous game of cat and mouse.
80. Two adventurers find love while searching for a legendary steam-powered artifact.
81. A young couple must navigate the challenges of a steam-powered society to be together.

82. A forbidden romance blooms between a nobleman and his steam-powered servant.
83. Two inventors collaborate on a project and discover their feelings for each other.
84. A steam-powered automaton struggles with its feelings for a human.
85. A romance develops between a scientist and their assistant while working on a groundbreaking invention.
86. A young engineer falls for the daughter of a powerful industrialist.
87. A love story unfolds between two passengers on a steam-powered airship.
88. A romance blossoms between two workers in a steam-powered lighthouse.
89. A detective and a criminal fall in love while playing a dangerous game of cat and mouse.
90. Two adventurers find love while searching for a legendary steam-powered artifact.
91. A young couple must navigate the challenges of a steam-powered society to be together.
92. A forbidden romance blooms between a nobleman and his steam-powered servant.
93. Two inventors collaborate on a project and discover their feelings for each other.
94. A steam-powered automaton struggles with its feelings for a human.
95. A romance develops between a scientist and their assistant while working on a groundbreaking invention.

96. A young engineer falls for the daughter of a powerful industrialist.
97. A love story unfolds between two passengers on a steam-powered airship.
98. A romance blossoms between two workers in a steam-powered lighthouse.
99. A detective and a criminal fall in love while playing a dangerous game of cat and mouse.
100. Two adventurers find love while searching for a legendary steam-powered artifact.

100 Political Intrigue and Espionage Prompts

1. A spy is sent to infiltrate a rival nation's steam-powered technology development.
2. A steam-powered device is at the center of a political scandal.
3. A steam-powered city's leader is assassinated, and a power struggle ensues.
4. A spy uncovers a plot to use steam-powered technology to destabilize the government.
5. A steam-powered automaton is used to gather intelligence for a secret organization.
6. A steam-powered airship is used to smuggle important documents out of a city.
7. A spy is tasked with stealing a blueprint for a new steam-powered weapon.
8. A steam-powered device is used to manipulate political elections.
9. A double agent is caught in a web of intrigue involving steam-powered technology.
10. A steam-powered factory is used as a front for a spy ring.

11. A steam-powered train carries a high-ranking official who is the target of an assassination plot.
12. A spy uses a steam-powered device to gather information on a rival nation's plans.
13. A steam-powered airship is used to transport a defecting scientist to safety.
14. A steam-powered device is used to eavesdrop on secret government meetings.
15. A spy uncovers a plot to use steam-powered technology to start a war.
16. A steam-powered factory worker is recruited to spy on their employer.
17. A steam-powered train is used to transport a dangerous prisoner who has valuable information.
18. A spy uses a steam-powered automaton to gather intelligence on a rival nation's activities.
19. A steam-powered airship is hijacked to steal important documents.
20. A steam-powered device is used to manipulate public opinion.
21. A double agent is caught in a web of intrigue involving steam-powered technology.
22. A steam-powered factory is used as a front for a spy ring.
23. A steam-powered train carries a high-ranking official who is the target of an assassination plot.

24. A spy uses a steam-powered device to gather information on a rival nation's plans.
25. A steam-powered airship is used to transport a defecting scientist to safety.
26. A steam-powered device is used to eavesdrop on secret government meetings.
27. A spy uncovers a plot to use steam-powered technology to start a war.
28. A steam-powered factory worker is recruited to spy on their employer.
29. A steam-powered train is used to transport a dangerous prisoner who has valuable information.
30. A spy uses a steam-powered automaton to gather intelligence on a rival nation's activities.
31. A steam-powered airship is hijacked to steal important documents.
32. A steam-powered device is used to manipulate public opinion.
33. A double agent is caught in a web of intrigue involving steam-powered technology.
34. A steam-powered factory is used as a front for a spy ring.
35. A steam-powered train carries a high-ranking official who is the target of an assassination plot.
36. A spy uses a steam-powered device to gather information on a rival nation's plans.
37. A steam-powered airship is used to transport a defecting scientist to safety.

38. A steam-powered device is used to eavesdrop on secret government meetings.
39. A spy uncovers a plot to use steam-powered technology to start a war.
40. A steam-powered factory worker is recruited to spy on their employer.
41. A steam-powered train is used to transport a dangerous prisoner who has valuable information.
42. A spy uses a steam-powered automaton to gather intelligence on a rival nation's activities.
43. A steam-powered airship is hijacked to steal important documents.
44. A steam-powered device is used to manipulate public opinion.
45. A double agent is caught in a web of intrigue involving steam-powered technology.
46. A steam-powered factory is used as a front for a spy ring.
47. A steam-powered train carries a high-ranking official who is the target of an assassination plot.
48. A spy uses a steam-powered device to gather information on a rival nation's plans.
49. A steam-powered airship is used to transport a defecting scientist to safety.
50. A steam-powered device is used to eavesdrop on secret government meetings.
51. A spy uncovers a plot to use steam-powered technology to start a war.

52. A steam-powered factory worker is recruited to spy on their employer.
53. A steam-powered train is used to transport a dangerous prisoner who has valuable information.
54. A spy uses a steam-powered automaton to gather intelligence on a rival nation's activities.
55. A steam-powered airship is hijacked to steal important documents.
56. A steam-powered device is used to manipulate public opinion.
57. A double agent is caught in a web of intrigue involving steam-powered technology.
58. A steam-powered factory is used as a front for a spy ring.
59. A steam-powered train carries a high-ranking official who is the target of an assassination plot.
60. A spy uses a steam-powered device to gather information on a rival nation's plans.
61. A steam-powered airship is used to transport a defecting scientist to safety.
62. A steam-powered device is used to eavesdrop on secret government meetings.
63. A spy uncovers a plot to use steam-powered technology to start a war.
64. A steam-powered factory worker is recruited to spy on their employer.

65. A steam-powered train is used to transport a dangerous prisoner who has valuable information.
66. A spy uses a steam-powered automaton to gather intelligence on a rival nation's activities.
67. A steam-powered airship is hijacked to steal important documents.
68. A steam-powered device is used to manipulate public opinion.
69. A double agent is caught in a web of intrigue involving steam-powered technology.
70. A steam-powered factory is used as a front for a spy ring.
71. A steam-powered train carries a high-ranking official who is the target of an assassination plot.
72. A spy uses a steam-powered device to gather information on a rival nation's plans.
73. A steam-powered airship is used to transport a defecting scientist to safety.
74. A steam-powered device is used to eavesdrop on secret government meetings.
75. A spy uncovers a plot to use steam-powered technology to start a war.
76. A steam-powered factory worker is recruited to spy on their employer.
77. A steam-powered train is used to transport a dangerous prisoner who has valuable information.

78. A spy uses a steam-powered automaton to gather intelligence on a rival nation's activities.
79. A steam-powered airship is hijacked to steal important documents.
80. A steam-powered device is used to manipulate public opinion.
81. A double agent is caught in a web of intrigue involving steam-powered technology.
82. A steam-powered factory is used as a front for a spy ring.
83. A steam-powered train carries a high-ranking official who is the target of an assassination plot.
84. A spy uses a steam-powered device to gather information on a rival nation's plans.
85. A steam-powered airship is used to transport a defecting scientist to safety.
86. A steam-powered device is used to eavesdrop on secret government meetings.
87. A spy uncovers a plot to use steam-powered technology to start a war.
88. A steam-powered factory worker is recruited to spy on their employer.
89. A steam-powered train is used to transport a dangerous prisoner who has valuable information.
90. A spy uses a steam-powered automaton to gather intelligence on a rival nation's activities.

91. A steam-powered airship is hijacked to steal important documents.
92. A steam-powered device is used to manipulate public opinion.
93. A double agent is caught in a web of intrigue involving steam-powered technology.
94. A steam-powered factory is used as a front for a spy ring.
95. A steam-powered train carries a high-ranking official who is the target of an assassination plot.
96. A spy uses a steam-powered device to gather information on a rival nation's plans.
97. A steam-powered airship is used to transport a defecting scientist to safety.
98. A steam-powered device is used to eavesdrop on secret government meetings.
99. A spy uncovers a plot to use steam-powered technology to start a war.
100. A steam-powered factory worker is recruited to spy on their employer.

100 Supernatural and Fantasy Prompts

1. A steam-powered city is haunted by the ghost of a former inventor.
2. A steam-powered device allows people to communicate with the dead.
3. A steam-powered automaton gains magical abilities.
4. A detective uses a steam-powered device to investigate supernatural occurrences.
5. A steam-powered airship encounters a dragon during its journey.
6. A steam-powered lighthouse is haunted by the ghost of its former keeper.
7. A steam-powered factory is the site of strange and unexplainable events.
8. A steam-powered ship encounters a sea monster during its voyage.
9. A steam-powered automaton is possessed by a vengeful spirit.
10. A steam-powered device allows people to see into the future.
11. A steam-powered city is plagued by a series of mysterious disappearances.

12. A steam-powered automaton becomes a vampire's assistant.
13. A steam-powered airship is used to hunt down mythical creatures.
14. A steam-powered lighthouse is the site of a ghostly apparition.
15. A steam-powered factory produces goods that have magical properties.
16. A steam-powered ship is used to transport a cursed artifact.
17. A steam-powered automaton becomes a witch's familiar.
18. A steam-powered device allows people to enter other dimensions.
19. A steam-powered city is protected by a group of magical guardians.
20. A steam-powered automaton is inhabited by a mischievous spirit.
21. A steam-powered airship is used to search for a lost magical kingdom.
22. A steam-powered lighthouse is the site of a supernatural event.
23. A steam-powered factory produces items that grant wishes.
24. A steam-powered ship is pursued by ghostly pirates.
25. A steam-powered automaton becomes a werewolf's companion.
26. A steam-powered device allows people to communicate with animals.

27. A steam-powered city is home to a secret society of wizards.
28. A steam-powered automaton is haunted by the spirit of its creator.
29. A steam-powered airship encounters a storm with magical properties.
30. A steam-powered lighthouse is the site of a haunting.
31. A steam-powered factory produces items that have supernatural abilities.
32. A steam-powered ship is used to search for a lost island filled with treasure.
33. A steam-powered automaton becomes a ghost hunter's assistant.
34. A steam-powered device allows people to control the elements.
35. A steam-powered city is threatened by a powerful sorcerer.
36. A steam-powered automaton is inhabited by a friendly spirit.
37. A steam-powered airship is used to transport a magical artifact.
38. A steam-powered lighthouse is the site of a ghostly encounter.
39. A steam-powered factory produces items that can change their appearance.
40. A steam-powered ship is pursued by a vengeful spirit.
41. A steam-powered automaton becomes a vampire's companion.

42. A steam-powered device allows people to see into the past.
43. A steam-powered city is home to a hidden magical academy.
44. A steam-powered automaton is haunted by the ghost of a former owner.
45. A steam-powered airship encounters a magical storm.
46. A steam-powered lighthouse is the site of a supernatural phenomenon.
47. A steam-powered factory produces items that can grant wishes.
48. A steam-powered ship is used to transport a cursed treasure.
49. A steam-powered automaton becomes a witch's assistant.
50. A steam-powered device allows people to communicate with the dead.
51. A steam-powered city is haunted by the ghost of a former ruler.
52. A steam-powered automaton gains magical abilities.
53. A detective uses a steam-powered device to investigate supernatural occurrences.
54. A steam-powered airship encounters a dragon during its journey.
55. A steam-powered lighthouse is haunted by the ghost of its former keeper.
56. A steam-powered factory is the site of strange and unexplainable events.

57. A steam-powered ship encounters a sea monster during its voyage.
58. A steam-powered automaton is possessed by a vengeful spirit.
59. A steam-powered device allows people to see into the future.
60. A steam-powered city is plagued by a series of mysterious disappearances.
61. A steam-powered automaton becomes a vampire's assistant.
62. A steam-powered airship is used to hunt down mythical creatures.
63. A steam-powered lighthouse is the site of a ghostly apparition.
64. A steam-powered factory produces goods that have magical properties.
65. A steam-powered ship is used to transport a cursed artifact.
66. A steam-powered automaton becomes a witch's familiar.
67. A steam-powered device allows people to enter other dimensions.
68. A steam-powered city is protected by a group of magical guardians.
69. A steam-powered automaton is inhabited by a mischievous spirit.
70. A steam-powered airship is used to search for a lost magical kingdom.
71. A steam-powered lighthouse is the site of a supernatural event.

72. A steam-powered factory produces items that grant wishes.
73. A steam-powered ship is pursued by ghostly pirates.
74. A steam-powered automaton becomes a werewolf's companion.
75. A steam-powered device allows people to communicate with animals.
76. A steam-powered city is home to a secret society of wizards.
77. A steam-powered automaton is haunted by the spirit of its creator.
78. A steam-powered airship encounters a storm with magical properties.
79. A steam-powered lighthouse is the site of a haunting.
80. A steam-powered factory produces items that have supernatural abilities.
81. A steam-powered ship is used to search for a lost island filled with treasure.
82. A steam-powered automaton becomes a ghost hunter's assistant.
83. A steam-powered device allows people to control the elements.
84. A steam-powered city is threatened by a powerful sorcerer.
85. A steam-powered automaton is inhabited by a friendly spirit.
86. A steam-powered airship is used to transport a magical artifact.

87. A steam-powered lighthouse is the site of a ghostly encounter.
88. A steam-powered factory produces items that can change their appearance.
89. A steam-powered ship is pursued by a vengeful spirit.
90. A steam-powered automaton becomes a vampire's companion.
91. A steam-powered device allows people to see into the past.
92. A steam-powered city is home to a hidden magical academy.
93. A steam-powered automaton is haunted by the ghost of a former owner.
94. A steam-powered airship encounters a magical storm.
95. A steam-powered lighthouse is the site of a supernatural phenomenon.
96. A steam-powered factory produces items that can grant wishes.
97. A steam-powered ship is used to transport a cursed treasure.
98. A steam-powered automaton becomes a witch's assistant.
99. A steam-powered device allows people to communicate with the dead.
100. A steam-powered city is haunted by the ghost of a former ruler.

100 War and Conflict Prompts

1. A steam-powered army invades a neighboring country.
2. A soldier uses a steam-powered exoskeleton in battle.
3. A steam-powered airship is used to transport troops to the front lines.
4. A steam-powered factory produces weapons for the war effort.
5. A spy uses a steam-powered device to gather intelligence on enemy movements.
6. A steam-powered train is used to transport soldiers and supplies to the battlefield.
7. A steam-powered ship is used to blockade an enemy port.
8. A steam-powered automaton is used as a weapon in battle.
9. A steam-powered airship is used to drop bombs on enemy targets.
10. A steam-powered factory is the target of a sabotage operation.
11. A steam-powered device is used to detect enemy movements.

12. A steam-powered lighthouse is used as a lookout post during a naval battle.
13. A steam-powered factory produces armor for soldiers.
14. A steam-powered train is used to evacuate civilians from a war zone.
15. A steam-powered ship is used to transport prisoners of war.
16. A steam-powered automaton is used to clear mines from a battlefield.
17. A steam-powered airship is used to deliver supplies to besieged troops.
18. A steam-powered factory produces ammunition for the war effort.
19. A steam-powered device is used to communicate with troops on the front lines.
20. A steam-powered lighthouse is used as a signal tower during a naval battle.
21. A steam-powered factory produces uniforms for soldiers.
22. A steam-powered train is used to transport wounded soldiers to a hospital.
23. A steam-powered ship is used to patrol a contested sea.
24. A steam-powered automaton is used as a scout in battle.
25. A steam-powered airship is used to evacuate wounded soldiers from the battlefield.
26. A steam-powered factory produces weapons for the war effort.

27. A steam-powered device is used to detect enemy communications.
28. A steam-powered lighthouse is used as a command center during a naval battle.
29. A steam-powered factory produces rations for soldiers.
30. A steam-powered train is used to transport reinforcements to the front lines.
31. A steam-powered ship is used to escort a convoy of supplies.
32. A steam-powered automaton is used to carry out sabotage missions behind enemy lines.
33. A steam-powered airship is used to conduct reconnaissance over enemy territory.
34. A steam-powered factory produces medical supplies for the war effort.
35. A steam-powered device is used to jam enemy communications.
36. A steam-powered lighthouse is used as a medical facility during a naval battle.
37. A steam-powered factory produces explosives for the war effort.
38. A steam-powered train is used to transport supplies to a besieged city.
39. A steam-powered ship is used to conduct a blockade of an enemy port.
40. A steam-powered automaton is used to deliver messages on the battlefield.
41. A steam-powered airship is used to deploy paratroopers behind enemy lines.

42. A steam-powered factory produces fuel for the war effort.
43. A steam-powered device is used to detect enemy mines.
44. A steam-powered lighthouse is used as a supply depot during a naval battle.
45. A steam-powered factory produces engines for military vehicles.
46. A steam-powered train is used to transport a high-ranking general to the front lines.
47. A steam-powered ship is used to conduct amphibious assaults on enemy positions.
48. A steam-powered automaton is used to provide medical aid on the battlefield.
49. A steam-powered airship is used to drop leaflets over enemy territory.
50. A steam-powered factory produces gas masks for soldiers.
51. A steam-powered device is used to intercept enemy communications.
52. A steam-powered lighthouse is used as a weapons storage facility during a naval battle.
53. A steam-powered factory produces vehicles for the war effort.
54. A steam-powered train is used to transport prisoners of war to a detention camp.
55. A steam-powered ship is used to conduct a naval blockade of an enemy port.
56. A steam-powered automaton is used to lay barbed wire on the battlefield.

57. A steam-powered airship is used to conduct night raids on enemy positions.
58. A steam-powered factory produces helmets for soldiers.
59. A steam-powered device is used to create false signals to confuse the enemy.
60. A steam-powered lighthouse is used as a command center during a naval battle.
61. A steam-powered factory produces artillery for the war effort.
62. A steam-powered train is used to transport spies behind enemy lines.
63. A steam-powered ship is used to conduct a naval blockade of an enemy port.
64. A steam-powered automaton is used to build fortifications on the battlefield.
65. A steam-powered airship is used to conduct psychological warfare against the enemy.
66. A steam-powered factory produces camouflage gear for soldiers.
67. A steam-powered device is used to create holographic decoys to confuse the enemy.
68. A steam-powered lighthouse is used as a radio station during a naval battle.
69. A steam-powered factory produces medical equipment for the war effort.
70. A steam-powered train is used to transport supplies to a remote outpost.
71. A steam-powered ship is used to conduct a naval blockade of an enemy port.

72. A steam-powered automaton is used to deliver supplies on the battlefield.
73. A steam-powered airship is used to conduct aerial photography over enemy territory.
74. A steam-powered factory produces gas masks for soldiers.
75. A steam-powered device is used to intercept enemy communications.
76. A steam-powered lighthouse is used as a medical facility during a naval battle.
77. A steam-powered factory produces explosives for the war effort.
78. A steam-powered train is used to transport supplies to a besieged city.
79. A steam-powered ship is used to conduct a blockade of an enemy port.
80. A steam-powered automaton is used to deliver messages on the battlefield.
81. A steam-powered airship is used to deploy paratroopers behind enemy lines.
82. A steam-powered factory produces fuel for the war effort.
83. A steam-powered device is used to detect enemy mines.
84. A steam-powered lighthouse is used as a supply depot during a naval battle.
85. A steam-powered factory produces engines for military vehicles.
86. A steam-powered train is used to transport a high-ranking general to the front lines.

87. A steam-powered ship is used to conduct amphibious assaults on enemy positions.
88. A steam-powered automaton is used to provide medical aid on the battlefield.
89. A steam-powered airship is used to drop leaflets over enemy territory.
90. A steam-powered factory produces gas masks for soldiers.
91. A steam-powered device is used to intercept enemy communications.
92. A steam-powered lighthouse is used as a weapons storage facility during a naval battle.
93. A steam-powered factory produces vehicles for the war effort.
94. A steam-powered train is used to transport prisoners of war to a detention camp.
95. A steam-powered ship is used to conduct a naval blockade of an enemy port.
96. A steam-powered automaton is used to lay barbed wire on the battlefield.
97. A steam-powered airship is used to conduct night raids on enemy positions.
98. A steam-powered factory produces helmets for soldiers.
99. A steam-powered device is used to create false signals to confuse the enemy.
100. A steam-powered lighthouse is used as a command center during a naval battle.

100 Exploration and Discovery Prompts

1. An explorer discovers a hidden steam-powered city in the jungle.
2. A steam-powered airship embarks on a journey to find a legendary lost civilization.
3. A steam-powered submarine explores the depths of the ocean in search of ancient artifacts.
4. An inventor creates a steam-powered device that reveals hidden treasures.
5. A team of adventurers sets out to map uncharted territories using steam-powered technology.
6. A steam-powered airship crew discovers a floating island in the sky.
7. An explorer uses a steam-powered exoskeleton to navigate a treacherous mountain range.
8. A steam-powered train is used to explore the uncharted regions of a desert.
9. A steam-powered ship sets sail to discover new lands across the ocean.

10. An inventor creates a steam-powered device that allows people to see through walls, revealing hidden passages.
11. A steam-powered airship is used to explore a mysterious, fog-covered island.
12. A team of scientists uses steam-powered technology to uncover the secrets of an ancient civilization.
13. An explorer discovers a steam-powered portal to another dimension.
14. A steam-powered submarine is sent to investigate a mysterious underwater city.
15. A steam-powered vehicle is used to traverse the dangerous terrain of a remote jungle.
16. An inventor creates a steam-powered device that can detect hidden treasures.
17. A steam-powered airship crew embarks on a journey to find a lost world.
18. A steam-powered train is used to explore the uncharted regions of a frozen wasteland.
19. A steam-powered ship sets sail to discover the source of a mysterious signal.
20. An explorer uses a steam-powered exoskeleton to navigate a dense forest.
21. A steam-powered airship is used to explore a series of uncharted islands.
22. A team of adventurers sets out to map the unknown regions of a vast desert.
23. A steam-powered submarine explores the depths of a sunken city.

24. An inventor creates a steam-powered device that reveals hidden tunnels.
25. A steam-powered airship crew discovers a lost civilization hidden in the clouds.
26. An explorer uses a steam-powered vehicle to traverse a dangerous volcanic landscape.
27. A steam-powered train is used to explore the uncharted regions of a remote wilderness.
28. A steam-powered ship sets sail to uncover the mysteries of an ancient island.
29. An inventor creates a steam-powered device that can see through solid objects, revealing hidden secrets.
30. A steam-powered airship is used to explore a forgotten temple in the jungle.
31. A team of scientists uses steam-powered technology to unlock the secrets of a lost world.
32. An explorer discovers a steam-powered gateway to another realm.
33. A steam-powered submarine is sent to investigate a mysterious underwater anomaly.
34. A steam-powered vehicle is used to navigate the treacherous terrain of an unknown continent.
35. An inventor creates a steam-powered device that can detect hidden chambers.
36. A steam-powered airship crew embarks on a journey to find a hidden paradise.

37. A steam-powered train is used to explore the uncharted regions of a vast mountain range.
38. A steam-powered ship sets sail to discover the secrets of a forgotten island.
39. An explorer uses a steam-powered exoskeleton to navigate a perilous canyon.
40. A steam-powered airship is used to explore a series of mysterious floating islands.
41. A team of adventurers sets out to map the unknown regions of a remote tundra.
42. A steam-powered submarine explores the depths of a hidden underwater cave.
43. An inventor creates a steam-powered device that reveals hidden doorways.
44. A steam-powered airship crew discovers a lost city in the sky.
45. An explorer uses a steam-powered vehicle to traverse a dangerous ice field.
46. A steam-powered train is used to explore the uncharted regions of a remote desert.
47. A steam-powered ship sets sail to uncover the mysteries of a lost civilization.
48. An inventor creates a steam-powered device that can see through fog, revealing hidden landscapes.
49. A steam-powered airship is used to explore a forgotten fortress in the mountains.
50. A team of scientists uses steam-powered technology to unlock the secrets of a hidden realm.

51. An explorer discovers a steam-powered portal to a parallel universe.
52. A steam-powered submarine is sent to investigate a mysterious underwater structure.
53. A steam-powered vehicle is used to navigate the treacherous terrain of an uncharted island.
54. An inventor creates a steam-powered device that can detect hidden relics.
55. A steam-powered airship crew embarks on a journey to find a mythical land.
56. A steam-powered train is used to explore the uncharted regions of a remote jungle.
57. A steam-powered ship sets sail to discover the secrets of a forgotten world.
58. An explorer uses a steam-powered exoskeleton to navigate a perilous swamp.
59. A steam-powered airship is used to explore a series of uncharted caverns.
60. A team of adventurers sets out to map the unknown regions of a vast forest.
61. A steam-powered submarine explores the depths of a hidden underwater grotto.
62. An inventor creates a steam-powered device that reveals hidden pathways.
63. A steam-powered airship crew discovers a lost kingdom in the sky.
64. An explorer uses a steam-powered vehicle to traverse a dangerous lava field.

65. A steam-powered train is used to explore the uncharted regions of a remote island.
66. A steam-powered ship sets sail to uncover the mysteries of a lost empire.
67. An inventor creates a steam-powered device that can see through darkness, revealing hidden dangers.
68. A steam-powered airship is used to explore a forgotten city in the mountains.
69. A team of scientists uses steam-powered technology to unlock the secrets of an ancient civilization.
70. An explorer discovers a steam-powered gateway to a hidden dimension.
71. A steam-powered submarine is sent to investigate a mysterious underwater anomaly.
72. A steam-powered vehicle is used to navigate the treacherous terrain of an unknown region.
73. An inventor creates a steam-powered device that can detect hidden passages.
74. A steam-powered airship crew embarks on a journey to find a hidden oasis.
75. A steam-powered train is used to explore the uncharted regions of a remote wilderness.
76. A steam-powered ship sets sail to discover the secrets of a forgotten island.
77. An explorer uses a steam-powered exoskeleton to navigate a perilous gorge.

78. A steam-powered airship is used to explore a series of uncharted fjords.
79. A team of adventurers sets out to map the unknown regions of a remote jungle.
80. A steam-powered submarine explores the depths of a hidden underwater canyon.
81. An inventor creates a steam-powered device that reveals hidden staircases.
82. A steam-powered airship crew discovers a lost palace in the clouds.
83. An explorer uses a steam-powered vehicle to traverse a dangerous glacier.
84. A steam-powered train is used to explore the uncharted regions of a remote valley.
85. A steam-powered ship sets sail to uncover the mysteries of a lost continent.
86. An inventor creates a steam-powered device that can see through sandstorms, revealing hidden treasures.
87. A steam-powered airship is used to explore a forgotten castle in the mountains.
88. A team of scientists uses steam-powered technology to unlock the secrets of a hidden kingdom.
89. An explorer discovers a steam-powered portal to an alternate reality.
90. A steam-powered submarine is sent to investigate a mysterious underwater ruin.
91. A steam-powered vehicle is used to navigate the treacherous terrain of an uncharted desert.

92. An inventor creates a steam-powered device that can detect hidden artifacts.
93. A steam-powered airship crew embarks on a journey to find a mythical city.
94. A steam-powered train is used to explore the uncharted regions of a remote tundra.
95. A steam-powered ship sets sail to discover the secrets of a forgotten land.
96. An explorer uses a steam-powered exoskeleton to navigate a perilous canyon.
97. A steam-powered airship is used to explore a series of uncharted caves.
98. A team of adventurers sets out to map the unknown regions of a remote mountain range.
99. A steam-powered submarine explores the depths of a hidden underwater lake.
100. An inventor creates a steam-powered device that reveals hidden vaults.

100 Science and Medicine Prompts

1. A steam-powered device is invented to cure a deadly disease, but it has unforeseen consequences.
2. A scientist creates a steam-powered exoskeleton to help the disabled walk again.
3. A steam-powered automaton is developed to perform complex surgeries.
4. A steam-powered airship is used to transport medical supplies to a remote region.
5. A steam-powered device is used to diagnose illnesses with incredible accuracy.
6. A steam-powered factory produces medical equipment for a groundbreaking new treatment.
7. A steam-powered train is used to transport patients to a specialized hospital.
8. A steam-powered ship is equipped with a state-of-the-art medical lab for research.
9. A steam-powered automaton is designed to provide care for the elderly.
10. A steam-powered device is invented to purify water and prevent disease.

11. A steam-powered airship is used to deliver vaccines to a remote village.
12. A steam-powered factory produces prosthetic limbs for war veterans.
13. A steam-powered train is used to transport a medical team to a disaster zone.
14. A steam-powered ship is used to quarantine patients during an outbreak.
15. A steam-powered automaton is developed to provide therapy for mental health patients.
16. A steam-powered device is invented to enhance human strength and endurance.
17. A steam-powered airship is used to conduct medical research in a remote region.
18. A steam-powered factory produces equipment for a new form of surgery.
19. A steam-powered train is used to transport medical supplies to a besieged city.
20. A steam-powered ship is used to conduct medical experiments at sea.
21. A steam-powered automaton is designed to assist doctors in the operating room.
22. A steam-powered device is invented to detect and remove toxins from the body.
23. A steam-powered airship is used to evacuate patients from a dangerous area.
24. A steam-powered factory produces machines for a revolutionary new treatment.
25. A steam-powered train is used to transport patients to a cutting-edge medical facility.

26. A steam-powered ship is equipped with a mobile hospital to treat patients at sea.
27. A steam-powered automaton is developed to provide care for terminally ill patients.
28. A steam-powered device is invented to accelerate the healing process.
29. A steam-powered airship is used to deliver medical aid to a war-torn region.
30. A steam-powered factory produces equipment for a new medical procedure.
31. A steam-powered train is used to transport a medical team to a remote village.
32. A steam-powered ship is used to conduct research on a new vaccine.
33. A steam-powered automaton is designed to provide physical therapy for injured soldiers.
34. A steam-powered device is invented to monitor vital signs and alert doctors to emergencies.
35. A steam-powered airship is used to transport organs for transplant.
36. A steam-powered factory produces machines for a new type of therapy.
37. A steam-powered train is used to transport medical supplies to a remote outpost.
38. A steam-powered ship is equipped with a lab to study infectious diseases.
39. A steam-powered automaton is developed to provide care for children with chronic illnesses.

40. A steam-powered device is invented to enhance human senses.
41. A steam-powered airship is used to conduct medical research in the Arctic.
42. A steam-powered factory produces equipment for a new form of diagnosis.
43. A steam-powered train is used to transport patients to a quarantine facility.
44. A steam-powered ship is used to study the effects of a new drug.
45. A steam-powered automaton is designed to assist in disaster relief efforts.
46. A steam-powered device is invented to treat psychological disorders.
47. A steam-powered airship is used to deliver medical supplies to a remote island.
48. A steam-powered factory produces machines for a new type of surgery.
49. A steam-powered train is used to transport medical staff to a crisis zone.
50. A steam-powered ship is used to quarantine patients during an epidemic.
51. A steam-powered automaton is developed to provide care for patients with rare diseases.
52. A steam-powered device is invented to regenerate damaged tissues.
53. A steam-powered airship is used to conduct medical research in a remote jungle.
54. A steam-powered factory produces equipment for a new form of therapy.

55. A steam-powered train is used to transport patients to a specialized treatment center.
56. A steam-powered ship is equipped with a lab to study the spread of diseases.
57. A steam-powered automaton is designed to provide care for the disabled.
58. A steam-powered device is invented to enhance human cognitive abilities.
59. A steam-powered airship is used to deliver medical aid to a disaster-stricken area.
60. A steam-powered factory produces machines for a new form of medical imaging.
61. A steam-powered train is used to transport medical supplies to a besieged town.
62. A steam-powered ship is used to conduct experiments on a new treatment.
63. A steam-powered automaton is developed to provide care for patients with chronic pain.
64. A steam-powered device is invented to detect and neutralize pathogens.
65. A steam-powered airship is used to conduct medical research in a remote desert.
66. A steam-powered factory produces equipment for a new form of surgery.
67. A steam-powered train is used to transport patients to a cutting-edge medical facility.
68. A steam-powered ship is equipped with a lab to study the effects of a new drug.
69. A steam-powered automaton is designed to assist in medical emergencies.

70. A steam-powered device is invented to treat neurological disorders.
71. A steam-powered airship is used to deliver medical supplies to a remote village.
72. A steam-powered factory produces machines for a new type of therapy.
73. A steam-powered train is used to transport medical staff to a crisis zone.
74. A steam-powered ship is used to quarantine patients during an outbreak.
75. A steam-powered automaton is developed to provide care for patients with rare conditions.
76. A steam-powered device is invented to regenerate organs.
77. A steam-powered airship is used to conduct medical research in a remote jungle.
78. A steam-powered factory produces equipment for a new form of therapy.
79. A steam-powered train is used to transport patients to a specialized treatment center.
80. A steam-powered ship is equipped with a lab to study the spread of infectious diseases.
81. A steam-powered automaton is designed to provide care for the elderly.
82. A steam-powered device is invented to enhance human physical abilities.
83. A steam-powered airship is used to deliver medical aid to a disaster-stricken area.
84. A steam-powered factory produces machines for a new form of medical treatment.

85. A steam-powered train is used to transport medical supplies to a besieged city.
86. A steam-powered ship is used to conduct experiments on a new vaccine.
87. A steam-powered automaton is developed to provide care for patients with chronic illnesses.
88. A steam-powered device is invented to detect and neutralize toxins.
89. A steam-powered airship is used to conduct medical research in a remote desert.
90. A steam-powered factory produces equipment for a new form of surgery.
91. A steam-powered train is used to transport patients to a cutting-edge medical facility.
92. A steam-powered ship is equipped with a lab to study the effects of a new treatment.
93. A steam-powered automaton is designed to assist in disaster relief efforts.
94. A steam-powered device is invented to treat psychological disorders.
95. A steam-powered airship is used to deliver medical supplies to a remote island.
96. A steam-powered factory produces machines for a new type of medical imaging.
97. A steam-powered train is used to transport medical staff to a crisis zone.
98. A steam-powered ship is used to quarantine patients during an epidemic.
99. A steam-powered automaton is developed to provide care for patients with chronic pain.

100.   A steam-powered device is invented to detect and treat infections.

100 Everyday Life Prompts

1. A family uses steam-powered appliances to make their daily lives easier.
2. A steam-powered device helps a student excel in their studies.
3. A steam-powered vehicle is used to commute to work in a bustling city.
4. A steam-powered gadget helps a chef create culinary masterpieces.
5. A steam-powered toy becomes a child's favorite companion.
6. A steam-powered device is used to clean the streets of a busy city.
7. A steam-powered clock tower keeps the entire city on schedule.
8. A steam-powered fountain becomes the centerpiece of a city park.
9. A steam-powered laundry machine revolutionizes household chores.
10. A steam-powered bicycle is used for daily transportation.
11. A steam-powered sewing machine creates beautiful garments.
12. A steam-powered printing press is used to publish the daily newspaper.

13. A steam-powered coffee machine becomes the talk of the town.
14. A steam-powered elevator makes it easier to navigate a tall building.
15. A steam-powered music box becomes a cherished family heirloom.
16. A steam-powered fan helps to cool a sweltering summer day.
17. A steam-powered loom weaves intricate patterns into fabric.
18. A steam-powered typewriter is used to write a best-selling novel.
19. A steam-powered water pump provides fresh water to a rural village.
20. A steam-powered garden tool makes tending to plants a breeze.
21. A steam-powered washing machine becomes a household necessity.
22. A steam-powered clock keeps perfect time in a bustling train station.
23. A steam-powered ice cream maker delights children and adults alike.
24. A steam-powered lawnmower makes yard work easy.
25. A steam-powered mail delivery system ensures letters arrive on time.
26. A steam-powered stove helps a baker create delicious pastries.
27. A steam-powered vacuum cleaner keeps a home spotless.

28. A steam-powered bath heater ensures a warm and relaxing soak.
29. A steam-powered record player fills a room with music.
30. A steam-powered printing press publishes the latest scientific discoveries.
31. A steam-powered hairdryer becomes a popular beauty tool.
32. A steam-powered dishwasher makes cleaning up after meals a breeze.
33. A steam-powered knitting machine creates cozy sweaters.
34. A steam-powered popcorn maker is a hit at movie nights.
35. A steam-powered toaster perfects the morning routine.
36. A steam-powered blender whips up delicious smoothies.
37. A steam-powered lamp brightens up a dark room.
38. A steam-powered clock keeps a classroom running smoothly.
39. A steam-powered pencil sharpener ensures perfect points every time.
40. A steam-powered juicer makes fresh fruit juice a daily treat.
41. A steam-powered heater keeps a home warm during winter.
42. A steam-powered radio broadcasts news and music to the masses.

43. A steam-powered waffle iron creates breakfast favorites.
44. A steam-powered doorbell alerts the household to visitors.
45. A steam-powered camera captures precious family moments.
46. A steam-powered baby stroller makes outings with infants easier.
47. A steam-powered pencil sharpener is a teacher's best friend.
48. A steam-powered ironing machine keeps clothes wrinkle-free.
49. A steam-powered flashlight lights the way during power outages.
50. A steam-powered curling iron creates stylish hairdos.
51. A steam-powered egg cooker ensures perfect breakfast every time.
52. A steam-powered stapler keeps papers organized.
53. A steam-powered water heater provides hot showers.
54. A steam-powered pet feeder ensures pets are fed on schedule.
55. A steam-powered bookbinding machine creates beautiful books.
56. A steam-powered bread maker fills the home with the smell of fresh bread.
57. A steam-powered treadmill keeps people fit and healthy.

58. A steam-powered toothbrush ensures clean teeth.
59. A steam-powered soap dispenser makes hand washing convenient.
60. A steam-powered juicer makes fresh fruit juice a daily treat.
61. A steam-powered heater keeps a home warm during winter.
62. A steam-powered radio broadcasts news and music to the masses.
63. A steam-powered waffle iron creates breakfast favorites.
64. A steam-powered doorbell alerts the household to visitors.
65. A steam-powered camera captures precious family moments.
66. A steam-powered baby stroller makes outings with infants easier.
67. A steam-powered pencil sharpener is a teacher's best friend.
68. A steam-powered ironing machine keeps clothes wrinkle-free.
69. A steam-powered flashlight lights the way during power outages.
70. A steam-powered curling iron creates stylish hairdos.
71. A steam-powered egg cooker ensures perfect breakfast every time.
72. A steam-powered stapler keeps papers organized.

73. A steam-powered water heater provides hot showers.

74. A steam-powered pet feeder ensures pets are fed on schedule.

75. A steam-powered bookbinding machine creates beautiful books.

76. A steam-powered bread maker fills the home with the smell of fresh bread.

77. A steam-powered treadmill keeps people fit and healthy.

78. A steam-powered toothbrush ensures clean teeth.

79. A steam-powered soap dispenser makes hand washing convenient.

80. A steam-powered juicer makes fresh fruit juice a daily treat.

81. A steam-powered heater keeps a home warm during winter.

82. A steam-powered radio broadcasts news and music to the masses.

83. A steam-powered waffle iron creates breakfast favorites.

84. A steam-powered doorbell alerts the household to visitors.

85. A steam-powered camera captures precious family moments.

86. A steam-powered baby stroller makes outings with infants easier.

87. A steam-powered pencil sharpener is a teacher's best friend.

88. A steam-powered ironing machine keeps clothes wrinkle-free.
89. A steam-powered flashlight lights the way during power outages.
90. A steam-powered curling iron creates stylish hairdos.
91. A steam-powered egg cooker ensures perfect breakfast every time.
92. A steam-powered stapler keeps papers organized.
93. A steam-powered water heater provides hot showers.
94. A steam-powered pet feeder ensures pets are fed on schedule.
95. A steam-powered bookbinding machine creates beautiful books.
96. A steam-powered bread maker fills the home with the smell of fresh bread.
97. A steam-powered treadmill keeps people fit and healthy.
98. A steam-powered toothbrush ensures clean teeth.
99. A steam-powered soap dispenser makes hand washing convenient.
100. A steam-powered juicer makes fresh fruit juice a daily treat.

100 Historical Figures and Events Prompts

1. A steam-powered device changes the course of a famous battle.
2. A historical figure uses a steam-powered invention to achieve greatness.
3. A steam-powered airship is used to rescue a famous explorer.
4. A steam-powered automaton assists a renowned scientist in their experiments.
5. A steam-powered train is used to transport a historical figure to a crucial meeting.
6. A steam-powered ship changes the outcome of a famous naval battle.
7. A steam-powered factory revolutionizes the industrial landscape.
8. A steam-powered device is used to save a historical landmark.
9. A steam-powered airship is used to explore uncharted territories.
10. A steam-powered automaton assists a famous artist in creating their masterpiece.
11. A steam-powered train is used to transport a delegation to a peace conference.

12. A steam-powered ship is used to discover new lands and cultures.
13. A steam-powered factory produces a groundbreaking new technology.
14. A steam-powered device is used to prevent a major disaster.
15. A steam-powered airship is used to transport supplies during a humanitarian crisis.
16. A steam-powered automaton assists a famous writer in their work.
17. A steam-powered train is used to transport troops during a critical battle.
18. A steam-powered ship is used to establish trade routes with distant lands.
19. A steam-powered factory produces goods that change the course of history.
20. A steam-powered device is used to uncover a long-lost treasure.
21. A steam-powered airship is used to transport a famous diplomat to a crucial negotiation.
22. A steam-powered automaton assists a renowned doctor in their medical practice.
23. A steam-powered train is used to transport a famous musician to their concert.
24. A steam-powered ship is used to explore the Arctic and discover new species.
25. A steam-powered factory produces a new form of energy that revolutionizes society.

26. A steam-powered device is used to decode an important message.
27. A steam-powered airship is used to transport supplies during a natural disaster.
28. A steam-powered automaton assists a famous engineer in their projects.
29. A steam-powered train is used to transport a famous athlete to their competition.
30. A steam-powered ship is used to rescue survivors of a shipwreck.
31. A steam-powered factory produces a new form of communication technology.
32. A steam-powered device is used to prevent an assassination attempt.
33. A steam-powered airship is used to transport a famous scientist to a crucial experiment.
34. A steam-powered automaton assists a renowned architect in their designs.
35. A steam-powered train is used to transport a famous actor to their performance.
36. A steam-powered ship is used to explore the depths of the ocean.
37. A steam-powered factory produces a new form of transportation.
38. A steam-powered device is used to uncover a hidden conspiracy.
39. A steam-powered airship is used to transport supplies during a famine.
40. A steam-powered automaton assists a famous inventor in their work.

41. A steam-powered train is used to transport a famous politician to a crucial debate.
42. A steam-powered ship is used to map the uncharted regions of the world.
43. A steam-powered factory produces a new form of entertainment.
44. A steam-powered device is used to save a historical figure from danger.
45. A steam-powered airship is used to transport a famous artist to their exhibition.
46. A steam-powered automaton assists a renowned musician in their performances.
47. A steam-powered train is used to transport a famous scientist to a groundbreaking experiment.
48. A steam-powered ship is used to discover new islands in the Pacific.
49. A steam-powered factory produces a new form of medicine.
50. A steam-powered device is used to prevent a major catastrophe.
51. A steam-powered airship is used to transport supplies during a war.
52. A steam-powered automaton assists a famous explorer in their adventures.
53. A steam-powered train is used to transport a famous author to their book signing.
54. A steam-powered ship is used to explore the depths of the Amazon River.
55. A steam-powered factory produces a new form of clothing.

56. A steam-powered device is used to uncover a hidden artifact.
57. A steam-powered airship is used to transport a famous doctor to a medical emergency.
58. A steam-powered automaton assists a renowned chef in their kitchen.
59. A steam-powered train is used to transport a famous diplomat to a peace summit.
60. A steam-powered ship is used to explore the uncharted regions of Antarctica.
61. A steam-powered factory produces a new form of energy.
62. A steam-powered device is used to prevent a historical event from being altered.
63. A steam-powered airship is used to transport supplies during a crisis.
64. A steam-powered automaton assists a famous artist in creating their masterpiece.
65. A steam-powered train is used to transport a famous politician to a crucial vote.
66. A steam-powered ship is used to establish new trade routes.
67. A steam-powered factory produces a new form of transportation.
68. A steam-powered device is used to decode an important message.
69. A steam-powered airship is used to transport a famous scientist to a critical experiment.

70. A steam-powered automaton assists a renowned doctor in their practice.
71. A steam-powered train is used to transport a famous musician to their concert.
72. A steam-powered ship is used to explore the depths of the ocean.
73. A steam-powered factory produces a new form of communication technology.
74. A steam-powered device is used to prevent an assassination attempt.
75. A steam-powered airship is used to transport supplies during a natural disaster.
76. A steam-powered automaton assists a famous engineer in their projects.
77. A steam-powered train is used to transport a famous athlete to their competition.
78. A steam-powered ship is used to rescue survivors of a shipwreck.
79. A steam-powered factory produces a new form of entertainment.
80. A steam-powered device is used to uncover a hidden conspiracy.
81. A steam-powered airship is used to transport a famous artist to their exhibition.
82. A steam-powered automaton assists a renowned musician in their performances.
83. A steam-powered train is used to transport a famous scientist to a groundbreaking experiment.
84. A steam-powered ship is used to explore the depths of the Amazon River.

85. A steam-powered factory produces a new form of clothing.
86. A steam-powered device is used to uncover a hidden artifact.
87. A steam-powered airship is used to transport a famous doctor to a medical emergency.
88. A steam-powered automaton assists a renowned chef in their kitchen.
89. A steam-powered train is used to transport a famous diplomat to a peace summit.
90. A steam-powered ship is used to explore the uncharted regions of Antarctica.
91. A steam-powered factory produces a new form of energy.
92. A steam-powered device is used to prevent a historical event from being altered.
93. A steam-powered airship is used to transport supplies during a crisis.
94. A steam-powered automaton assists a famous artist in creating their masterpiece.
95. A steam-powered train is used to transport a famous politician to a crucial vote.
96. A steam-powered ship is used to establish new trade routes.
97. A steam-powered factory produces a new form of transportation.
98. A steam-powered device is used to decode an important message.

99. A steam-powered airship is used to transport a famous scientist to a critical experiment.
100. A steam-powered automaton assists a renowned doctor in their practice.

100 Environmental Themes Prompts

1. A steam-powered device is invented to clean polluted rivers.
2. A steam-powered airship is used to study the effects of climate change.
3. A steam-powered factory converts waste into usable energy.
4. A steam-powered train transports environmental scientists to a remote research station.
5. A steam-powered ship is used to monitor ocean health.
6. A steam-powered automaton plants trees to combat deforestation.
7. A steam-powered device is used to reduce air pollution.
8. A steam-powered airship delivers supplies to an eco-friendly community.
9. A steam-powered factory produces biodegradable products.
10. A steam-powered train is used to transport renewable energy resources.
11. A steam-powered ship cleans up oil spills in the ocean.

12. A steam-powered automaton monitors wildlife populations.
13. A steam-powered device is used to recycle waste materials.
14. A steam-powered airship is used to study endangered species.
15. A steam-powered factory produces sustainable building materials.
16. A steam-powered train transports solar panels to a remote village.
17. A steam-powered ship is used to track migrating whales.
18. A steam-powered automaton restores damaged ecosystems.
19. A steam-powered device is used to purify polluted air.
20. A steam-powered airship is used to deliver clean water to drought-stricken areas.
21. A steam-powered factory produces eco-friendly packaging.
22. A steam-powered train transports wind turbines to a new wind farm.
23. A steam-powered ship is used to study the effects of overfishing.
24. A steam-powered automaton cleans up plastic waste from the ocean.
25. A steam-powered device is used to monitor carbon emissions.
26. A steam-powered airship is used to reforest a barren landscape.

27. A steam-powered factory produces organic farming equipment.
28. A steam-powered train transports researchers to study a melting glacier.
29. A steam-powered ship is used to explore the Great Barrier Reef.
30. A steam-powered automaton assists in wildlife conservation efforts.
31. A steam-powered device is used to generate renewable energy.
32. A steam-powered airship is used to study the effects of deforestation.
33. A steam-powered factory produces compostable products.
34. A steam-powered train transports clean energy to a remote town.
35. A steam-powered ship monitors the health of coral reefs.
36. A steam-powered automaton plants crops in arid regions.
37. A steam-powered device is used to track endangered animals.
38. A steam-powered airship delivers eco-friendly technology to a developing country.
39. A steam-powered factory produces sustainable fashion.
40. A steam-powered train transports electric cars to a city.
41. A steam-powered ship is used to study the impact of climate change on sea levels.

42. A steam-powered automaton restores wetlands.
43. A steam-powered device is used to capture and store carbon emissions.
44. A steam-powered airship is used to deliver renewable energy solutions.
45. A steam-powered factory produces green energy equipment.
46. A steam-powered train transports environmental activists to a protest.
47. A steam-powered ship is used to study marine life in the Arctic.
48. A steam-powered automaton cleans up polluted soil.
49. A steam-powered device is used to monitor global warming.
50. A steam-powered airship is used to replant forests after a wildfire.
51. A steam-powered factory produces eco-friendly household items.
52. A steam-powered train transports scientists to study a protected wildlife area.
53. A steam-powered ship is used to remove ghost nets from the ocean.
54. A steam-powered automaton monitors the health of ecosystems.
55. A steam-powered device is used to filter pollutants from the air.
56. A steam-powered airship delivers educational materials about sustainability.

57. A steam-powered factory produces renewable energy devices.
58. A steam-powered train transports eco-tourists to a nature reserve.
59. A steam-powered ship is used to study the effects of acidification on marine life.
60. A steam-powered automaton plants vegetation to prevent soil erosion.
61. A steam-powered device is used to measure and reduce water waste.
62. A steam-powered airship is used to support sustainable agriculture projects.
63. A steam-powered factory produces biodegradable electronics.
64. A steam-powered train transports conservationists to a remote habitat.
65. A steam-powered ship monitors the health of the Antarctic ecosystem.
66. A steam-powered automaton assists in habitat restoration projects.
67. A steam-powered device is used to generate clean energy from waste.
68. A steam-powered airship is used to deliver solar energy kits to off-grid communities.
69. A steam-powered factory produces eco-friendly transportation solutions.
70. A steam-powered train transports renewable energy experts to a summit.
71. A steam-powered ship is used to map the effects of climate change on the oceans.

72. A steam-powered automaton helps to clean polluted rivers.
73. A steam-powered device is used to improve waste management.
74. A steam-powered airship supports reforestation initiatives.
75. A steam-powered factory produces products that reduce environmental impact.
76. A steam-powered train transports clean energy solutions to a disaster-stricken area.
77. A steam-powered ship is used to monitor the impact of human activity on marine life.
78. A steam-powered automaton plants trees in urban areas.
79. A steam-powered device is used to enhance recycling processes.
80. A steam-powered airship delivers technology for sustainable living.
81. A steam-powered factory produces materials that reduce carbon footprints.
82. A steam-powered train transports researchers to study renewable energy sources.
83. A steam-powered ship is used to explore the impact of pollution on marine environments.
84. A steam-powered automaton helps to rebuild ecosystems after natural disasters.
85. A steam-powered device is used to create sustainable energy solutions.

86. A steam-powered airship supports conservation efforts in remote areas.
87. A steam-powered factory produces tools for environmental monitoring.
88. A steam-powered train transports climate scientists to critical research sites.
89. A steam-powered ship is used to study the impact of climate change on polar regions.
90. A steam-powered automaton restores habitats damaged by human activity.
91. A steam-powered device is used to mitigate the effects of pollution.
92. A steam-powered airship delivers resources for sustainable development.
93. A steam-powered factory produces products that promote environmental health.
94. A steam-powered train transports renewable energy equipment to developing areas.
95. A steam-powered ship monitors the impact of industrial activity on marine life.
96. A steam-powered automaton plants vegetation to combat desertification.
97. A steam-powered device is used to optimize resource conservation.
98. A steam-powered airship supports sustainable living initiatives.
99. A steam-powered factory produces innovations that reduce environmental harm.
100. A steam-powered train transports environmental advocates to global summits.

100 Mysteries and Puzzles Prompts

1. A steam-powered device holds the key to solving a centuries-old mystery.
2. A detective uses a steam-powered gadget to uncover a hidden treasure.
3. A steam-powered airship crash reveals a hidden map to an ancient artifact.
4. A steam-powered automaton is the only one who knows the solution to a cryptic puzzle.
5. A steam-powered train is the setting for a mysterious disappearance.
6. A steam-powered ship's crew must solve riddles to escape a cursed island.
7. A steam-powered factory hides a secret room with a mysterious object.
8. A steam-powered device reveals a hidden message that leads to a treasure hunt.
9. A steam-powered airship's logbook contains clues to an unsolved crime.
10. A steam-powered automaton deciphers an ancient language that holds a secret.
11. A steam-powered train transports a mysterious package that everyone wants to steal.

12. A steam-powered ship's captain is murdered, and the crew must find the killer.
13. A steam-powered factory worker discovers a secret code in the machinery.
14. A steam-powered device is used to unlock a hidden safe with valuable contents.
15. A steam-powered airship is hijacked, and the passengers must solve puzzles to regain control.
16. A steam-powered automaton is programmed to reveal a secret only when certain conditions are met.
17. A steam-powered train's schedule holds the key to solving a complex puzzle.
18. A steam-powered ship's compass points to a hidden island with a mysterious history.
19. A steam-powered factory is the setting for a series of unexplained events.
20. A steam-powered device helps a detective solve a locked-room mystery.
21. A steam-powered airship's cargo holds clues to a long-lost civilization.
22. A steam-powered automaton is the keeper of a family's dark secrets.
23. A steam-powered train's conductor is found dead, and the passengers must find the culprit.
24. A steam-powered ship's journal reveals a map to a hidden treasure.
25. A steam-powered factory's blueprints hide a secret that someone is willing to kill for.

26. A steam-powered device is the key to solving a series of robberies.
27. A steam-powered airship's route reveals clues to a hidden vault.
28. A steam-powered automaton is programmed to solve an ancient riddle.
29. A steam-powered train's passengers are involved in a high-stakes game of deception.
30. A steam-powered ship's logs lead to an underwater treasure.
31. A steam-powered factory's inventor is found dead, and the workers must solve the mystery.
32. A steam-powered device holds the secret to a powerful family's fortune.
33. A steam-powered airship's crew uncovers a conspiracy involving a lost artifact.
34. A steam-powered automaton assists in deciphering a series of cryptic messages.
35. A steam-powered train's route is the key to uncovering a hidden network of tunnels.
36. A steam-powered ship's captain leaves a trail of clues to a hidden treasure.
37. A steam-powered factory is the setting for a mysterious disappearance.
38. A steam-powered device is used to solve a series of puzzles in an ancient tomb.
39. A steam-powered airship's blueprints hold clues to a secret invention.
40. A steam-powered automaton is the key to unlocking a hidden library of knowledge.

41. A steam-powered train's cargo holds a valuable artifact that everyone wants.
42. A steam-powered ship's crew must solve a series of puzzles to escape a pirate's curse.
43. A steam-powered factory's owner is found dead, and the workers must find the murderer.
44. A steam-powered device reveals a hidden message that leads to a lost city.
45. A steam-powered airship's passengers must work together to solve a mystery.
46. A steam-powered automaton is programmed with the location of a hidden treasure.
47. A steam-powered train's route reveals clues to a series of unsolved crimes.
48. A steam-powered ship's logbook contains a code that leads to a hidden island.
49. A steam-powered factory's machinery holds a secret that someone is willing to kill for.
50. A steam-powered device is the key to solving a high-profile kidnapping.
51. A steam-powered airship's crew discovers a hidden chamber with a mysterious object.
52. A steam-powered automaton assists in solving a series of complex puzzles.
53. A steam-powered train's passengers are involved in a conspiracy to steal a valuable artifact.
54. A steam-powered ship's captain leaves a series of riddles that lead to a hidden treasure.

55. A steam-powered factory is the setting for a series of unexplained accidents.
56. A steam-powered device helps a detective solve a series of murders.
57. A steam-powered airship's blueprints reveal the location of a hidden vault.
58. A steam-powered automaton is programmed to reveal a secret only when certain conditions are met.
59. A steam-powered train's schedule holds the key to solving a complex puzzle.
60. A steam-powered ship's compass points to a hidden island with a mysterious history.
61. A steam-powered factory is the setting for a series of unexplained events.
62. A steam-powered device helps a detective solve a locked-room mystery.
63. A steam-powered airship's cargo holds clues to a long-lost civilization.
64. A steam-powered automaton is the keeper of a family's dark secrets.
65. A steam-powered train's conductor is found dead, and the passengers must find the culprit.
66. A steam-powered ship's journal reveals a map to a hidden treasure.
67. A steam-powered factory's blueprints hide a secret that someone is willing to kill for.
68. A steam-powered device is the key to solving a series of robberies.

69. A steam-powered airship's route reveals clues to a hidden vault.
70. A steam-powered automaton is programmed to solve an ancient riddle.
71. A steam-powered train's passengers are involved in a high-stakes game of deception.
72. A steam-powered ship's logs lead to an underwater treasure.
73. A steam-powered factory's inventor is found dead, and the workers must solve the mystery.
74. A steam-powered device holds the secret to a powerful family's fortune.
75. A steam-powered airship's crew uncovers a conspiracy involving a lost artifact.
76. A steam-powered automaton assists in deciphering a series of cryptic messages.
77. A steam-powered train's route is the key to uncovering a hidden network of tunnels.
78. A steam-powered ship's captain leaves a trail of clues to a hidden treasure.
79. A steam-powered factory is the setting for a mysterious disappearance.
80. A steam-powered device is used to solve a series of puzzles in an ancient tomb.
81. A steam-powered airship's blueprints hold clues to a secret invention.
82. A steam-powered automaton is the key to unlocking a hidden library of knowledge.
83. A steam-powered train's cargo holds a valuable artifact that everyone wants.

84. A steam-powered ship's crew must solve a series of puzzles to escape a pirate's curse.
85. A steam-powered factory's owner is found dead, and the workers must find the murderer.
86. A steam-powered device reveals a hidden message that leads to a lost city.
87. A steam-powered airship's passengers must work together to solve a mystery.
88. A steam-powered automaton is programmed with the location of a hidden treasure.
89. A steam-powered train's route reveals clues to a series of unsolved crimes.
90. A steam-powered ship's logbook contains a code that leads to a hidden island.
91. A steam-powered factory's machinery holds a secret that someone is willing to kill for.
92. A steam-powered device is the key to solving a high-profile kidnapping.
93. A steam-powered airship's crew discovers a hidden chamber with a mysterious object.
94. A steam-powered automaton assists in solving a series of complex puzzles.
95. A steam-powered train's passengers are involved in a conspiracy to steal a valuable artifact.
96. A steam-powered ship's captain leaves a series of riddles that lead to a hidden treasure.
97. A steam-powered factory is the setting for a series of unexplained accidents.

98. A steam-powered device helps a detective solve a series of murders.
99. A steam-powered airship's blueprints reveal the location of a hidden vault.
100. A steam-powered automaton is programmed to reveal a secret only when certain conditions are met.

100 Artistic and Creative Prompts

1. A steam-powered automaton becomes a renowned artist.
2. A steam-powered device allows musicians to play instruments with unprecedented skill.
3. A steam-powered airship is transformed into a traveling art gallery.
4. A steam-powered factory produces materials for an innovative new art form.
5. A steam-powered train is used to transport a famous orchestra on tour.
6. A steam-powered ship is used as a floating theater for performances.
7. A steam-powered automaton is programmed to compose symphonies.
8. A steam-powered device allows sculptors to create intricate masterpieces.
9. A steam-powered airship is used to transport a world-famous ballet company.
10. A steam-powered factory produces pigments for vibrant paintings.
11. A steam-powered train transports a traveling circus with amazing acts.
12. A steam-powered ship is used to stage an opera at sea.

13. A steam-powered automaton becomes a famous playwright.
14. A steam-powered device allows artists to paint with light.
15. A steam-powered airship is used to host an international art festival.
16. A steam-powered factory produces fabrics for extravagant costumes.
17. A steam-powered train transports a famous theater troupe on tour.
18. A steam-powered ship is used to showcase a renowned sculptor's work.
19. A steam-powered automaton is programmed to dance ballet.
20. A steam-powered device allows writers to produce books at incredible speeds.
21. A steam-powered airship is transformed into a mobile music studio.
22. A steam-powered factory produces paper for a famous writer.
23. A steam-powered train is used to transport a famous painter's works to an exhibition.
24. A steam-powered ship is used to host a floating art school.
25. A steam-powered automaton becomes a world-class chef.
26. A steam-powered device allows photographers to capture images in new ways.
27. A steam-powered airship is used to film a groundbreaking movie.

28. A steam-powered factory produces materials for innovative architecture.
29. A steam-powered train transports a famous dancer to a prestigious competition.
30. A steam-powered ship is used to host a renowned fashion show.
31. A steam-powered automaton is programmed to create beautiful mosaics.
32. A steam-powered device allows actors to perform with unprecedented realism.
33. A steam-powered airship is used to document the creation of a massive mural.
34. A steam-powered factory produces instruments for a famous orchestra.
35. A steam-powered train transports a renowned poet on a reading tour.
36. A steam-powered ship is used to host a floating film festival.
37. A steam-powered automaton becomes a famous choreographer.
38. A steam-powered device allows writers to visualize their stories in 3D.
39. A steam-powered airship is transformed into a giant canvas for a painter.
40. A steam-powered factory produces materials for experimental theater.
41. A steam-powered train is used to transport a famous composer's works to a concert hall.
42. A steam-powered ship is used to stage a floating ballet.

43. A steam-powered automaton is programmed to create stunning stained glass.
44. A steam-powered device allows musicians to compose music with unprecedented speed.
45. A steam-powered airship is used to host a worldwide dance competition.
46. A steam-powered factory produces materials for innovative sculptures.
47. A steam-powered train transports a renowned author on a book tour.
48. A steam-powered ship is used to stage a floating art exhibition.
49. A steam-powered automaton becomes a celebrated novelist.
50. A steam-powered device allows painters to create works of art with light.
51. A steam-powered airship is transformed into a mobile theater.
52. A steam-powered factory produces fabrics for avant-garde fashion.
53. A steam-powered train is used to transport a famous artist's works to a gallery.
54. A steam-powered ship is used to host a floating music festival.
55. A steam-powered automaton is programmed to create intricate jewelry.
56. A steam-powered device allows sculptors to carve with unprecedented precision.
57. A steam-powered airship is used to host an international film festival.

58. A steam-powered factory produces materials for innovative architecture.
59. A steam-powered train transports a famous dancer to a prestigious competition.
60. A steam-powered ship is used to host a renowned fashion show.
61. A steam-powered automaton is programmed to create beautiful mosaics.
62. A steam-powered device allows actors to perform with unprecedented realism.
63. A steam-powered airship is used to document the creation of a massive mural.
64. A steam-powered factory produces instruments for a famous orchestra.
65. A steam-powered train transports a renowned poet on a reading tour.
66. A steam-powered ship is used to host a floating film festival.
67. A steam-powered automaton becomes a famous choreographer.
68. A steam-powered device allows writers to visualize their stories in 3D.
69. A steam-powered airship is transformed into a giant canvas for a painter.
70. A steam-powered factory produces materials for experimental theater.
71. A steam-powered train is used to transport a famous composer's works to a concert hall.
72. A steam-powered ship is used to stage a floating ballet.

73. A steam-powered automaton is programmed to create stunning stained glass.
74. A steam-powered device allows musicians to compose music with unprecedented speed.
75. A steam-powered airship is used to host a worldwide dance competition.
76. A steam-powered factory produces materials for innovative sculptures.
77. A steam-powered train transports a renowned author on a book tour.
78. A steam-powered ship is used to stage a floating art exhibition.
79. A steam-powered automaton becomes a celebrated novelist.
80. A steam-powered device allows painters to create works of art with light.
81. A steam-powered airship is transformed into a mobile theater.
82. A steam-powered factory produces fabrics for avant-garde fashion.
83. A steam-powered train is used to transport a famous artist's works to a gallery.
84. A steam-powered ship is used to host a floating music festival.
85. A steam-powered automaton is programmed to create intricate jewelry.
86. A steam-powered device allows sculptors to carve with unprecedented precision.
87. A steam-powered airship is used to host an international film festival.

88. A steam-powered factory produces materials for innovative architecture.
89. A steam-powered train transports a famous dancer to a prestigious competition.
90. A steam-powered ship is used to host a renowned fashion show.
91. A steam-powered automaton is programmed to create beautiful mosaics.
92. A steam-powered device allows actors to perform with unprecedented realism.
93. A steam-powered airship is used to document the creation of a massive mural.
94. A steam-powered factory produces instruments for a famous orchestra.
95. A steam-powered train transports a renowned poet on a reading tour.
96. A steam-powered ship is used to host a floating film festival.
97. A steam-powered automaton becomes a famous choreographer.
98. A steam-powered device allows writers to visualize their stories in 3D.
99. A steam-powered airship is transformed into a giant canvas for a painter.
100. A steam-powered factory produces materials for experimental theater.